**ISLINGTON**

Please return this item on or before the last date stamped below or you may be liable to overdue charges. To renew an item call the number below, or access the online catalogue at www.islington.gov.uk/libraries. You will need your library membership number and PIN number.

5|17

D1347815

Islington Libraries

020 7527 6900   **www.islington.gov.uk/libraries**

whole and complete. It is certainly worthy of your time and attention."

— ZEN MASTER DENNIS GENPO MERZEL,

author of *Big Mind, Big Heart*

"Enza's book is a true book in that it continually brings the attention to what is the immediacy, the actuality right now, the uncontrived spontaneous naturalness. Being constantly reminded in various ways in every chapter that there is only life essence (awareness), the believed-in entity is seen to have no self-nature and not stand on its own. In this recognition the book has done its work and that is That."

— SAILOR BOB ADAMSON, author of *What's Wrong with Right Now Unless You Think About It?*

"Enza writes in such a clear and down-to-earth way that it is almost impossible not to be able to relate to what she is pointing to. She describes how every child already knows their true nature and how simple it really is, and encourages the reader to check what is really true in their own experience rather than blindly believing what they have been taught since they have 'grown up'. Reading her wonderful book was just like drinking a nice cool drink that goes down so very easily. It is the validation that so many people are longing to hear."

— UNMANI LIZA HYDE, author of *Die to Love*

INSTANT PRESENCE

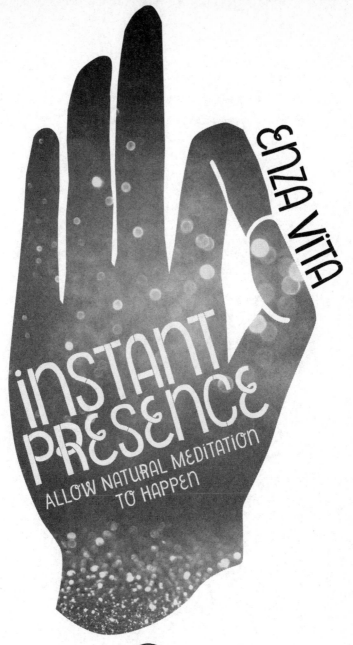

ENZA VITA

INSTANT PRESENCE

ALLOW NATURAL MEDITATION TO HAPPEN

WATKINS

Sharing Wisdom Since
1893

This edition first published in the UK and USA 2017 by

Watkins, an imprint of Watkins Media Limited

19 Cecil Court

London WC2N 4EZ

enquiries@watkinspublishing.com

Design and typography copyright © Watkins Media Limited 2017

Text copyright © Enza Vita 2017

10 9 8 7 6 5 4 3 2 1

Printed and bound in Europe

A CIP record for this book is available from the British Library

ISBN: 978-1-786780-61-4

www.watkinspublishing.com

To Awareness,
the only reality living through everything
as everything
and to you, dear reader,
may you realize your already existing freedom

CONTENTS

Acknowledgements xi

Foreword by Lama Surya Das xiii

Introduction 1

Prologue 9

PART 1: THE SEARCH FOR ENLIGHTENMENT 17

    1.   What is Enlightenment? 19

    2.   Realizing What You Are Not, Recognizing What You Are 29

    3.   Simple Ordinary Awareness. 43

PART 2: PRACTICE OR NO PRACTICE, AND WHICH PRACTICE? 57

    4.   Truth is That Which Knows the Way 59

    5.   Real Meditation is Letting Go of Control 69

    6.   Allowing Natural Meditation to Happen 79

PART 3: FLIP-FLOPPING – LOSING AND FINDING YOURSELF ... 91

7.   The Seduction of Thought 97

8.   The Sway of Emotion............................. 107

9.   Become the Sky 115

PART 4: LIVING THE TRUTH OF WHO WE ARE 125

10.   To Die Before We Die 129

11.   Live Where You Fear to Live...................... 139

12.   We Taste Only Sacredness....................... 147

Epilogue: Be As You Are..................................... 161

Interview with Enza Vita 167

A Secret Sky Within 179

About the Author 181

ACKNOWLEDGEMENTS

I offer heartfelt thanks to my partner, Leo. Without your encouragement, this book would never have happened.

Thanks also to Shanti Einolander for your loving and very patient editing. Thank you for your invaluable suggestions and feedback that helped to turn a bunch of notes I had been writing and collecting over the years into a book.

Finally, I offer a deep bow of love and gratitude to all the amazing teachers who have guided and inspired me on my path. I owe you a huge debt of gratitude and every day I offer all that is bright and joyful in my life at your feet, because without you, I would never have had the ability to appreciate it and recognize it.

FOREWORD

by Lama Surya Das

BEING (T)HERE WHILE GETTING THERE, EVERY STEP OF THE WAY

The inherent freedom and completeness of authentic *being* is the radiant, beating heart of our Tibetan Dzogchen lineage. Enza well knows this way of being and how it expresses and manifests itself as naturalness and spontaneous *doing* without pushing, striving or resistance and inhibition. We say that *nowness–awareness, or the immediacy of pure presence* (of Mind, of Self), is the heart-essence of enlightenment, the innate wakefulness at the centre of our existence, even in sleep or coma.

To awaken to this makes all the difference, and liberates oneself on the spot. Awaken from what? Awaken from illusion, confusion and delusion; realizing autonomy within interconnectedness, not just a teenager's half-baked idea of independence and freedom. As if carrying one's own atmosphere wherever one goes and whatever happens, it's a complete paradigm shift, a figure-ground turnaround from the small self to the supreme Self, from small thinking mind to non-conceptual Buddha-Mind; from feeling like a mere cog in the wheel or a grain of sand in the universe, to the already complete and perfect wholeness and completion we call in Tibetan, The Natural Great Perfection – that luminous primordial awareness directly intuiting that all is complete as it is and should and must be.

The Hevajra Tantra scripture of Vajrayana (tantric) Buddhism spells it out: "We are all Buddhas by nature. It is only adventitious obscurations which veil that fact." The sole task is to awaken to who and what we truly are. This is the essence of enlightenment and the luminous, numinous heart of the Dharma.

Enza's personal awakening story is worth the price of admission. Enlightened wisdom is like an endangered natural resource today, which we overlook at our peril; let's join in exploring our true identity and developing our own innate transformational resources for a change. When I become clearer, everything becomes clearer. This great work unveils this profound understanding, as well as how to penetrate it and integrate it into daily life.

I myself had long wondered if enlightenment or total wakefulness was real or even possible. Is there a *there* there, and where and what could it be like? Who knows, actualizes and genuinely embodies this sublime truth, this universal gnosis or transcendental wisdom woven throughout the mystical traditions of the perennial philosophy? It turns out to be truer than I could have conceived. Anyone can become awakened, and even enlightened, similar to what the historical teacher named Buddha realized, as well as sages throughout the ages. There is a *there* there, and it is right here! Who knew? *Being (t)here while getting there* is the heart of the secret wrapped in a koan inside a mystery, which only the beyond-conceptual mind can penetrate.

Pre-eminent Zen master of Japan, Hakuin, long ago sang:

"This land where we stand is the Pure Land, paradise; this body the body of Buddha."

He don't mean Japan, or his body, but yours, mine, ours. Wake up, help yourself. *Live authentically.*

INTRODUCTION

I sit here looking out, filled with an emptiness that spills over and keeps on spilling. There is no end to this boundlessness, this delicious thrill of *Presence*.

Nothing can contain it, for everything is contained within it. The good and the bad, the black and the white, the harsh and the gentle – simply flavours of *Its* passage.

Here, here, always here. So simple, so immediate. This is always here.

Call it whatever you will. In truth, *This* has no name. Too exquisite to speak of, too delicate to touch, delicious, tender, yet so very solid, vast, fathomless.

All that exists comes out of *This*. All that exists returns to *This*. No one owns *This*, yet everyone belongs to *This*.

*   *   *

This endless well of delight was first revealed to me in 2007, when the imaginary shell containing what I thought I was broke open, revealing what had always been here.

I had always believed I was this concrete separate entity called Enza, living in a big old world, and now the world was in me. I was literally filled with the world, which included the body–mind called Enza.

All ideas about higher or lower selves, all the inner debates about practice or no practice, enlightenment or non-enlightenment, were gone. Now there was only *this*, totally different from what I had imagined. No mind could have imagined this.

Ever since I could remember I had been addicted to the idea of "spiritual awakening". At different times in my life I had been engaged in that idea through meditation, reading hundreds of spiritual books, trying to be "present", questioning my belief systems, and waiting for the moment when the separate self would disappear and with it all my suffering. With the exception of a few wonderful but fleeting experiences, I did not get the awakening I had hoped for until the day when it simply unveiled itself, revealing that it had never actually been hidden.

The searching for "it" outside myself had separated me from the very thing I was seeking. That day I discovered that I was already a part of it and that life was already and had always been complete.

I am often asked what has changed since that day. In truth, nothing at all has changed – nothing except the viewpoint and, with that, everything changes. Now, life is no longer lived through the lens of a separate individual or one who is seeking anything other than what is right here. I am no longer interested in chasing special states because I am happy with what is here now.

Freedom includes all and it is not separate from our everyday dualistic existence, including ordinary thoughts, feelings and perceptions.

The mundane activities of eating, walking and breathing are now spacious openness, pure presence expressing itself in the world. My greatest misunderstanding in the past was to be so focused on attaining the transcendental that I was constantly overlooking the obvious in the most ordinary moment, right here, right now.

Now, my experience is more like when I was a child. As children, before the ego becomes solidified, we are just simply present and we are not yet identified with living in time and space, a past and a future.

As I sit here writing this, I have absolutely no idea where the words are coming from, who is doing it or what it all means. Life is simply lived in this present moment, allowing for this human manifestation to maintain its role in the world while no longer believing in the finite, limited perspectives of "self" and "world" that our minds create.

I still work as the editor/publisher of a holistic newspaper, meeting deadlines and gathering news and stories. I still prepare meals for my family and do the washing and cleaning. I still journey through emotions and thoughts that naturally arise through my day-to-day interactions with the world, yet all of this no longer holds me captive. I am no longer identified as a separate entity that is doing any of this. The thoughts and emotions that come and go I now know are not my thoughts or emotions, and in this knowingness, there is freedom.

It's not that I have changed into someone more patient, less reactive or more perfect; it's just that now I have released my investment in all of that. There is no longer any anxiety about non-perfection, neither is there credit for so-called successes or failures.

Now I simply respond to the world around me and allow for the next moment to arise. And in this natural response to the world, I see everything in it as a part of what I really am. Life requests action ... and so I act. Life requests stillness ... and so I am still. This is not a passiveness to the delicate touch of the moment, but an intimate engagement, allowing each moment to be just as it is. No longer searching for the "why" and the "how", I simply breathe, look, listen and allow.

There is no end to this allowing. It is an ongoing deepening as I slowly lose more and more of what I think I am. Sometimes this allowing is blissful, sometimes it is painful, yet through it all there is this wakefulness, the clarity and aliveness that wasn't noticed before, and this is life. Real life. Through this act of allowing, this book started to take shape.

I had been writing for a few years, mostly as a way of helping me to clarify what was unfolding inside me. One day my partner, Leo, asked me to share some of my writings with him and then suggested I consider getting them published. At first I felt some resistance. How would I ever be able to fully communicate my experience? But as the allowing deepened and the doubts began to dissolve, I was left only with what life was asking of me.

Some of the content in this book comes from personal journals, some of it originates from responses to questions asked by family, friends and individuals who follow my blogs – questions regarding enlightenment and the recognition of one's true self.

You will find that some phrases, concepts and ideas keep repeating themselves throughout the book. In truth, every moment is a fresh opportunity to open to what is, as it is. Each moment is a fresh call to actually see what is truly here, what all of manifest reality is actually arising in.

Just as life offers us infinite opportunities to re-awaken to our true nature, use each repetition in this book to once again inquire into the reality that is being pointed to. The invitation is to look deeper than the words to *that which is looking*. Then each repetition becomes a doorway to see anew what is always already present and free within you.

There will also be moments when you feel drawn to pause and reflect upon a particular point of inquiry that has a strong resonance for you. This is awareness calling. These moments are doorways to Truth, right here, right now. Welcome them. Stay open and receptive to the inner nudges and give them your full presence, for they are infinitely precious.

The book is divided into four parts and at the end of each part you will encounter a "Presence Pause" that is signalled like this:

PRESENCE PAUSE

There you will find various contemplations and lines of inquiry that will point you to a direct encounter with your enlightened nature. At these points I encourage you to put the book down and contemplate what life is whispering.

You might also consider keeping an ongoing journal of self-inquiry while reading the book. Participating in this way will begin to invite this awareness into your daily life, where there is infinite opportunity for clear seeing. This seeing is really the only practice necessary, not only to awaken, but also to clarify and embody this awakening. To practise Instant Presence simply means to be internally still and undistracted, leaving your experience of the moment (including thoughts, sights, sounds and sensations) as it is, without trying to improve it, correct it or replace it. This is not a passive surrender but a letting go to being totally present and totally relaxed.

As you read these pages, please understand that I don't have anything you don't already possess. What you are searching for is what you already are. You are always already free.

This book's purpose is not to give you more knowledge, more concepts, more beliefs or more practices, but to help point you back to that which shines eternally within you, needing nothing for the revelation of itself. May you come to know, without a doubt, that who you truly are is this freedom. This has always been and always will be so.

All that exists is this freedom, and you are *all*. You are the awake, boundless, omnipresent consciousness that is right here, right now.

To follow where I am pointing is to abandon all that you know – all your experiences, all your concepts, all your states and conditions — and jump into the unknown. It is to free yourself from all reference points, all limitations and all boundaries. To let go of all hope for a better, more spiritual future for yourself.

The reaching for enlightenment is the last thing this "me" you believe yourself to be does just before it dissolves into pure awareness, your natural original state.

Join me now on a journey to where you already are, this placeless place you have never really left.

PROLOGUE

Although dwelling on the past has nothing to do with the message in this book, a little history may explain how it came about and put it into context. However, please remember that enlightenment is not an experience. Whatever experiences we may come across in our spiritual journey, we are not any of those experiences, but rather the one who is witnessing them, the pure awareness cognizing them without thought.

The experience may be of bliss, of silence, even of nothingness, but it is not what we are. We are the experiencing of it.

We must leave all experiences behind, and keep going to the point where every object goes — silence, bliss, nothingness, until there is nothing left but our own subjectivity. Then, no bliss is more blissful, no silence deeper, no nothingness truer.

DEEPER THAN BLISS

It was the last day of a meditation retreat, and for a few days I had been unable to sleep as a familiar wave of energy ran up and down my body. It felt as if I was plugged into an immense source of energy. Even though I was functioning on very little sleep, I awakened that morning feeling good.

The bell rang, announcing the first meditation session of the day. I sat on a chair at the back of the meditation room and took a deep breath in and out. I let myself relax into the cushion, while being careful to maintain an alert presence. Over the previous few months I had been working at maintaining a balance between relaxation and 360-degree openness all around, while at the same time being alertly aware. Too much relaxation and I would fall asleep; too much alertness and I would become agitated.

After a few minutes into the session, a huge rush of energy began rising within the centre of my body. The feeling was so incredibly powerful that it frightened me.

My gut reaction was to open my eyes and look toward the meditation teacher. I could distinguish her facial features, but I had to focus hard to keep her face from floating away. I took a deep breath and closed my eyes again, trying to settle with the energy that was now shaking my body. Then a thought floated by in consciousness: "What is perceiving this?"

With my eyes still closed, I sensed a movement arising from a vast bottomless chasm. As I began to focus my attention on it, it appeared as though I was looking into a reflective surface.

A shiver of terror went down my spine as I realized that what I was seeing was actually myself moving. Not the self I was familiar with, but something so endlessly vast, totally unexpected, infinitely unimaginable and so utterly terrifying that my mind gave up. I disappeared into a nothingness with no-thing in it. No forms, no sounds, no thoughts and no self – just absolute nothingness.

The next thing I was aware of was the bell signalling the end of the sitting meditation and the beginning of the walking meditation. I found it difficult to comprehend anything. I couldn't remember my name or who I was. I got up and went outside.

The world appeared different. The trees shimmered vibrantly in iridescent hues. Everything was extremely clear and had a sense of immediacy. Every little thing was alive and present. At this point I laughed, overtaken by joy.

My joy turned to awe as I began to sense a breathtaking presence. It was incredibly vast, bright and alive, yet also personal, intimate and intense, radiating pure love everywhere. It was harmonious. It was infinite. It was unimaginable. It was perfect.

Another meditator approached and asked me about a salad she was preparing. Without any effort, the answer rolled off my tongue. To my surprise, she didn't notice anything different about me. To her, I still appeared to be a normal and coherent woman, even though I still could not recall my own name. I found this so funny that I had to keep myself from laughing out aloud. I didn't feel ready to give a reason for my sudden bout of laughter because I was not sure she would understand.

Gradually the experience subsided and by nightfall, I was back to normal reality again, back in name and identification. In my bed that night, I reflected on my experience. While I felt indescribable gratitude for it, I sensed that the experience I'd just had was not complete. If it had ended, it could not have been the "real thing". I knew that there was still something that I wasn't fully seeing.

Since I was a child I'd had many spiritual experiences like this, and they all had a beginning, middle and an end. They were always about "me" having "my" experience. I intuitively knew that what I was looking for was not only before and beyond time and space, but also before and beyond any ideas of self.

EFFORTLESS FRUIT

The next day I woke up feeling very sick, and lay in bed for a month, too weak to move. Then, as suddenly as it had come, the sickness left and I decided to go out for a bit of fresh air.

I was walking down the street when suddenly I realized I was not existing in the individual shell that had once encased my personality so tightly. The person I'd once thought of as me, rigidly held together and kept separate from other individual existences, had melted into something indescribable, an infinite space containing everything and giving rise to everything.

I was that space, I was everything in it, and I was the awareness of it, yet the space and what appeared within the space were not "two". Since there was no line to distinguish between "my" awareness and the images I saw, I realized that this experience was not happening to a personal self. Both appearances were simply in and of awareness and whatever perceived this was awareness itself.

Everything appeared very normal, very ordinary, and yet something was different. I was not having thoughts; I was what contained the thoughts. The same was true for all appearances including emotions, states, sensations and experiences. Everything was appearing and disappearing within the space that I am. There were no boundaries or borders.

I was everywhere and everything – the mid-afternoon sky, the sound of my boots hitting the footpath and the chewing gum sticking to them.

I was every blade of grass, every bird that flew across the sky and the rubbish bin waiting to be collected.

I was also the body–mind called Enza, all of it; body, sensations, feelings and thoughts were still experienced, but only within this wholeness, as an aspect of this wholeness.

And I saw that this awareness had always been here, I had always been *this*. This "me" included not only infinite space but also everything in the past, everything in the future and all of time. Amazingly I had never noticed it before, because by searching for it outside myself, I had continuously overlooked it.

WHY TALK OF ANYTHING ELSE?

At first I avoided speaking about this to anyone, having decided that I was not going to share my "experience". At the time it seemed better to keep quiet, partly because I believed I would not be able to fully communicate it and partly because the history of the entity I had believed to be me was one of not wanting to do anything that made her overly visible. If I were to start talking about this, it was bound to happen that others would project their notions onto me. I knew that I may be met with scepticism and that some would question my intentions. But slowly, as the stronghold on this mind-generated identity started to loosen its grip, I became more willing to do whatever life wanted of me, including the writing of this book if it could help others to recognize their true nature as that which is always and already, completely and naturally *free*.

PART 1

THE SEARCH FOR ENLIGHTENMENT

"IF YOU ARE UNABLE TO FIND TRUTH RIGHT WHERE YOU
ARE, WHERE ELSE DO YOU EXPECT TO FIND IT?"
– DŌGEN

Most of us live our lives in a continuous state of moving toward happiness and away from pain. We believe what we have is never enough, and our continual efforts to grasp the "next best thing" that we think will make us happy inevitably leads to suffering.

As long as we continue to see happiness as a state that can only be found by getting something outside of ourselves, as long as we continue to experience endless cycles of acceptance and rejection, desiring and not desiring, pushing in one direction and pulling in another, we will never experience lasting happiness.

Living in a three-dimensional world makes us believe in the illusion that there is a "me" in direct opposition to an "other" that is outside of us. This "other" can be people, places, circumstances and objects of all kinds.

It's hard for us to view the world in any other way but this one.

The search for happiness will be never-ending as long as we believe there is a "me" in here and an "everything else" out there. Suffering is guaranteed to continue as long as we insist on viewing the world in these dualistic terms.

At some point in our personal journeys, we start to see the impossibility of such a dualistic set-up. We want to be free of the paradox. We want an end to our suffering. We hear about this thing called "enlightenment" and we think, "Aha, this will be my ticket out!" and so begins the search for enlightenment.

But what is this elusive state called enlightenment?

1

WHAT IS ENLIGHTENMENT?

A SPIRITUAL SEEKER ASKED ZEN MASTER ZOKETSU
"IS THERE A FULLY ENLIGHTENED MASTER HERE?"
"I SURE HOPE NOT" THE ZEN MASTER REPLIED WITHOUT
MISSING A BEAT. "WE HAVE ENOUGH TROUBLE ALREADY."
– A ZEN STORY

The Sanskrit word Bodhi, often translated as "enlightenment", actually means "awakened". Awakened from what? In essence, from the trance of believing that we are separate individuals, apart from all that is. It is clearly seeing who and what we truly are, and what we are not.

Another word for enlightenment or awakening is "awareness". Not awareness of something in particular, but an awakening to pure awareness itself.

It has been said that after the Buddha attained enlightenment, a man passing him on the road was stunned by his magnificent radiance and peaceful countenance. Stopping before the Buddha the man asked, "You are surely a God?"

The Buddha answered, "No."

"Then you must be a magician? A sorcerer? A wizard?"

"No."

"You must be some kind of celestial being then? Are you an angel?"

Again, the Buddha simply said, "No."

"So, what are you then?" the man asked.

"I am awake," the Buddha replied.

The word Buddha, in fact, means "the one who is awake". The term applies not just to Siddhārtha Gautama, but also to all other Buddhas (awakened human beings) who have realized this awakeness.

WHAT DOES IT MEAN TO BE AWAKE?

Dōgen, in the "Genjōkōan", said, "To carry oneself forward and experience myriad things is delusion. That myriad things come forth and experience themselves is awakening."

The first phrase, "To carry oneself forward and experience myriad things is delusion" is about seeing things from our own individual point of view. If I'm "here" watching and interpreting things "out there", then this is delusion.

The next phrase, "That myriad things come forth and experience themselves is awakening", is about everything, including the body–mind, being a part of this great painting, arising and dissolving every moment. This is awakening.

WHERE DO YOU HAVE TO GO TO FIND ENLIGHTENMENT?

Typically, we go looking "out there". We are like the farmer who owns a horse, yet forgets that the horse is already in its stable, so he goes off searching for it.

We look outside ourselves because we imagine that there is some great cosmic experience to be found out there, somewhere in the "sacred" world. We feel that our normal ordinary consciousness is too simple and too mundane to be meaningful. Just seeing a bird or a tree in our backyard is too ordinary to mean much.

So maybe we go searching in India, or in the Himalayas, or in caves and monasteries, or endless self-help workshops and spiritual retreats. And while we may find other awakened people in these places, we won't necessarily find our own enlightened nature.

Why? Because, like the horse that is already in its stable, our own enlightened nature has never gone anywhere; we just continue to miss it, to overlook it, simply because we are looking everywhere except in the most obvious place; right at home, right here in this present ordinary moment.

THE ONLY WAY TO GET HOME IS TO RECOGNIZE THAT WE ARE ALREADY THERE

Those who are actively seeking enlightenment will not find it because the act of looking for it is the distraction from it.

The idea that we can become enlightened implies that this is not already so, that we are not free enough or complete enough, that we are a limited being with a problem, and that problem is that we are not enlightened.

This is in complete contradiction to the basic position of the great non-duality traditions that say that there is a reality and "thou art that". I invite you to search long and hard in these traditions to try to find anything suggesting that we need to "become" that or even to "deepen into that".

All of the world's greatest spiritual teachings say the same thing:

"I and the Father are One."

"You are That."

"Your own mind is Buddha Mind."

"The eye by which I see God is the eye by which God sees me."

Do you recognize these phrases?

Many people expend much effort trying to remove what they believe to be obstacles to enlightenment, all the while never realizing that the first and largest obstacle is the belief that there is an obstacle. The second largest obstacle is the belief that it's difficult and you have to struggle to reach it.

What is needed is to take all the energy and attention that goes into maintaining those beliefs and shift it to turning the attention back toward itself. This means we can simply stop, pause and be still, not entertaining any thoughts or beliefs. We can actually turn the energy around, turn it inward and be present with ourselves.

Just by stopping all those cluttering thoughts and ideas, we begin to tap into that stillness and into what is here and now in the present moment.

ONLY HERE, ONLY NOW

Truly, we don't need to pack our bags and go searching for ourselves in a monastery or in someone else's backyard. What we are looking for is always already here, looking through our eyes, hearing through our ears and feeling through our hearts. It can only be found right where we are, as our own perceiving awareness, not separate from what is perceived.

What we are is not an altered state, but an innocent, original, unmodified stateless state. Many of us are trying to get enlightened and have ideas of merging with the cosmos or experiencing great energetic states, but those are altered states.

Many seekers are searching, purifying, growing and so on. Years later, they are still doing the same thing because they do not realize that they have bought into a conceptual prison with no exit.

*   *   *

If we have never left our true home, why do we forget and struggle to find our way back in?

Who can say for sure? Some traditions say that God is playing games with Itself just for the fun of losing and finding Itself. Others say that being born in this human form causes us to lose touch with who we are.

Many years ago, the Persian mystic poet, Rumi, described in one of his poems his own realization with this paradox of searching for the place we already stand in: *"I have lived on the lip of insanity, wanting to know reasons, knocking on a door. It opens. I've been knocking from the inside."*

This poem mirrors the surprise and delight that many seekers feel when they discover after years of desperate searching that they have never been apart, even for an instant, from the home they have been seeking for so long.

Rumi describes this realization as "the door opening". This "opening" is the recognition that "It's always me, interacting with me." The freedom that comes with the opening of the door is the freedom of recognition (which in Latin means to know again – to re-cognate).

Keep searching if you must, keep enquiring, but knock only once. Then open up and notice. Not only does the door open, but you open the door to yourself.

* * *

Are you enlightened and how do you know that you have realized? How can you be sure of it?

It may sound contradictory, but I can't say I'm enlightened or unenlightened. Neither statement is a lie. Nobody arrived and yet something did. What did? Nothing!

Being enlightened ironically means realizing that there is no separate entity that can be enlightened or unenlightened. This is a realization that cannot be laid claim to by a specific individual because in that moment the individual is no longer there.

At the moment of enlightenment, everything is dropped – body, mind, all states, all things – everything. At that moment, there is no separate entity that can become enlightened, because there is no "*I*" that can experience it.

How do you know when you have had a good meal? You know because your stomach is full and you are satisfied. Realization is similar to that. You have swallowed everything. You have swallowed the entire world. Everything is in your own consciousness now.

You don't need others to tell you this fact, or for others to recognize this fact, or even to approve it. Whether others believe you or not, it doesn't matter, because your stomach is full and you need nothing else.

*   *   *

Can a teacher or guru help me to realize my true nature? And how would I go about choosing one?

There is only one teacher, your inner teacher, and that is awareness. My suggestion is that you stay with that one. The true guru is a manifestation of your true nature, as it exists internally and appears to exist externally. The true guru is actually you made manifest, not the you that you think you are but the real you, awareness itself. Since who you truly are is the totality of being, you are capable of generating many forms, both human and non-human, to bring the focus of the illusionary seeker back to itself.

"Guru" is really another word for awareness.

In regard to the human teacher, be guided, first of all, by love. Follow your heart and see where it takes you. If one day you meet someone in whose company you find you can be yourself, and if you feel clear, peaceful, happy, and your mind becomes calm for no apparent reason, you may like to keep his or her company from time to time.

Jean Klein, a well-known speaker and author on the subject of non-duality, said, "You will know a true teacher because you will feel yourself, in your autonomy, in his or her presence." With the true teacher you are free to be yourself rather than bound by rules and agendas. The true teacher doesn't take the identity and role of the teacher seriously and has no need for his/her students to feel complete.

The greatness of a teacher is not in psychic powers, lineages, credentials, in the number of followers, eloquence, intellect or charisma. Greatness is the extent to which the vehicle has been taken over by the realization and has ceased grasping.

When you meet such a teacher, there is actually nobody there. Apart from thoughts and concepts of a separate self, there is nobody there in you either.

In reality there is no difference between you and the guru, as there is no difference between the space in this cup and the space in that cup. The cup cannot limit the all-pervasive space.

Ultimately, there are no teachers or teachings because there aren't any students. There is only ever unconditional awareness – Oneness meeting Itself as That.

2

REALIZING WHAT YOU ARE NOT, RECOGNIZING WHAT YOU ARE

"YOUR WHOLE IDEA ABOUT YOURSELF IS BORROWED,
BORROWED FROM THOSE WHO HAVE NO IDEA
OF WHO THEY ARE THEMSELVES."
– DZOGCHEN PONLOP

When I was seven or eight years old, I was sitting playing on the floor of my house near the front door, which had been left half-open. Rays of sunlight filtered through the open door, surrounding me and casting pools of light on the floor. Particles of dust danced on the beams of light, and I extended my hand to touch them.

I knew that the rays were connected all the way to the sun in the sky and I felt that by touching a piece of the sun shining on the pavement of my house, I was touching the sun itself. Something about this realization thrilled me, and I could feel the sunlight rushing through my body, lighting every cell. Looking at the sunlight streaming in, I could feel every detail. I was the sunshine, a bright and warm ray of light, and thousands of particles danced within me.

Suddenly my awareness shifted to the top of the door where the light entered, and I saw a spider sitting very still in its web just outside the door. For a moment I was the spider, as well as its web of fine threads moving in the wind and I could feel the sunlight warming my body.

I heard a sound and my awareness was pulled upward to see a little brown bird sitting on the power lines above the house. I was the bird. I ruffled my feathers and flew toward a pink flower cascading from the balcony across the street.

Then a breath arose, and suddenly I was a child of flesh and blood again.

As children, we know effortlessly that our nature is awareness and that we are one with all that is. Now, as an adult, the possibility is for this aware presence that we have always been our whole life, and which we are right now, to suddenly become aware of itself.

AWAKENESS IS INHERENT
IN ALL THINGS

There are two approaches to realizing our true nature. The first is to discover the truth of who we are. The second is to discover what we are not.

These two approaches are actually the same thing, two ways of expressing the same idea. If we get rid of the false thoughts of who we think we are, the remainder is what we really are. And when we realize what we really are, all thoughts of who we thought we were drop away and we are free from the suffering of misidentification.

The famous Indian sage Nisargadatta Maharaj once said, "You can either push the cart or pull the cart. Both are fine as long as you keep the cart rolling!"

WHO OR WHAT ARE YOU REALLY?

Who are you really and how do you answer this seemingly easy question? Do you answer it with your name, your family history or your professional title? Or, do you answer it with your role as a mother, a father, a daughter, a son, a husband, a wife, a lover?

Any answer the mind comes up with is just another story about who we think we are: our hobbies, what we like, what we don't like, what we have accomplished, what we haven't accomplished, how we grew up, our talents and abilities, and so on. The answers never stop changing. They are constantly in flux. This is the human experience. We are always thinking about, adjusting and developing who we imagine ourselves to be in order to get along in society, to comprehend the reasons behind our actions, or to get ready for something new that is about to happen. However, not a single answer or all of them combined can provide a complete definition of what we are.

At some point you realize that none of these ideas of who you are provide an adequate answer, and it's at this point that you may find yourself at the edge of a vast open space wondering, "Can this be who I am?" And then the next thought: "No, impossible, there's nothing here." The mind cannot comprehend this vast nothingness, and so what usually happens is that we turn back to what we were doing before the question arose.

The only purpose to the question, "Who am I?" is to point us back to that which is already looking through our eyes, listening through our ears, thinking through our thoughts, and feeling through our hearts.

NOTICING WHAT NEVER CHANGES

There is an aspect of you that has accompanied you through all of your life experiences as your very nature. This you is the same you that was peering through your eyes when you were a baby, a child, a teenager and throughout your adulthood.

Thoughts, emotions, beliefs, ideas, practices and mental states have all come and gone endlessly, but the fundamental experience of beingness remains always constant, always steady, always here. Can you identify what it is that is perpetually unmoving and always present?

Right now, for the purpose of investigation, let's take a moment to observe your thoughts. Notice also the beliefs, emotions and body sensations forming and dissipating. These are all simply phenomena that come and go. They are not permanent. As such, they are fundamentally unable to be a part of your true self, which is eternal.

Anything that appears and disappears cannot actually be you because it is being observed by you. By removing the attention from these things and noticing what remains, you are left only with what is permanent – the truth of who you are.

As thoughts, ideas, emotions, beliefs, belongings and events come and go, notice that there is an aware and awake intelligence that remains permanent and unchanging even as thoughts and ideas continue to form and dissolve and the world around you continues to change. You are aware of all of it forming, just as you are aware of all of it dissipating.

Once your attention is off all that changes, only this awakeness remains. At any moment you can turn your attention directly to this aware presence, awareness is that which is reading these words right now, whatever "that" is. You know without a doubt that there is something reading these words right now and awareness is precisely what that is. You are this awake intelligence that is aware of every idea, every emotion and every event.

WASH YOURSELF OF YOURSELF

One of the mistakes we can still make at this point is that when attention wanders into thoughts and then imagines a thinking "me", a conglomerate of beliefs is born, and like a cloud hides the sun, those ideas appear to hide this aware presence.

All that is really happening is that the attention has wandered into thinking. The only thing that could appear to conceal our original nature is our thinking.

Reverse the attention 180 degrees to that which thinking arises from and appears upon, and you will see yourself.

The only thing that is required of you is to stop identifying who you are with the many forms that awareness takes. As soon as you stop identifying with form, which is the "content" of awareness, then all that is left is pure awareness, *you*.

Wise men and women from time immemorial have talked about an "all-embracing ultimate reality", which is none other than your very own ordinary present awareness. Try not to stray from this profound simplicity.

THE BRILLIANT CLARITY OF EVER-PRESENT AWARENESS

When you are viewing a TV show and the screen suddenly goes blank, all that is left is the television screen itself and then you become aware that you've been so mesmerized by the programme, you forgot that you were looking at a screen. The images and stories kept your attention so engrossed that you'd forgotten that without the screen, the images you were viewing wouldn't even be there.

Awareness is exactly like this. It is the television screen upon which all impermanent experiences, perceptions and thoughts are projected. As you withdraw attention from the distraction of thought, you become aware of the screen of awareness.

When you have had enough practice viewing the "blank screen" of awareness without attention flowing into thoughts, you will then begin to be able to sense it in the background even when your mind is full of thoughts.

THE SUN LOOKING FOR THE LIGHT

Awareness, our true nature, is like the sun in the sky. The sun's rays are the pathless path we travel back and forth between our original nature and its expression, thoughts, emotions and objects. Without encountering an object, the light of the sun wouldn't be visible. It is only visible when it reflects off an object.

Manifest reality, the world around us, is the object, a mirror-like reality that reflects back the sun, allowing its light to be seen. Just as a reflection in the mirror, it may look very real, but it is only a reflection. Although it might look like there are two realities, the sun and the mirror, there is really only One. This One is absolute spaciousness and this spaciousness includes everything, keeps everything within its embrace, and lovingly lets all things exist in whatever way they choose.

What happens in this space does not corrupt or debase it. Everything in existence emerges from and falls back into this pure, immaculate and incorruptible space; be it emotions like pain and anger, battles and armed conflicts, despotic dictators, all manifestations of weather including rain, wind, snow and the clouds that float across the sky, as well as the people in our lives whom we cherish the most.

The "you" that you think you are also arises in this space that you are.

AWARENESS IS OPEN, TRANSPARENT AND ALWAYS AWARE OF ITSELF

Just be aware of the sense of presence that is always here. Now, don't think about what you have just read. Simply notice the awakeness that is seeing the world through your eyes now and is always seeing the world through your eyes. This seeing is timeless and never leaves you. What is looking is this pure awareness. The truth of who you are is this actual awareness, which has always been free. Anything else, all concepts of what you are, are only thoughts appearing and disappearing in the brightly aware space that you are.

Once you realize this, you get the divine joke of it all, and there is often laughter and a joy unlike anything you have ever known. You see that what you have been looking for everywhere is what you have always been. Nothing can change this fact nor improve upon it in any way. So what does this leave you with? What is there to do? Not much. You have found everything you need.

It's like searching for Rome. Once you finally arrive in the centre of your longed-for destination, do you enjoy it or do you immediately go running off somewhere else? Every thought you entertain of any other place only takes you one step away from Rome. Any movement you make takes you away from where you have finally arrived. So you have to be willing to stop right then and there! Once you understand your real position, you see you do not need to go anywhere else. No matter what you do, anywhere else you might go, it is never going to bring you any closer to where you already are.

*   *   *

Can you explain the difference between mind and awareness and how they express in the human being? How do you recognize these two states in yourself? And does the mind need to be purified before it can recognize awareness?

The mind holds on to subject/object duality. It grabs everything it likes, rejects what it doesn't, and is indifferent to the rest.

Awareness manifests in the body–mind as a "feeling" of being wide open, 360 degrees on all sides, while being aware. This is not a mentally fabricated openness because if it were, it would be lost as soon as you forget to keep it in mind.

That which recognizes awareness is not the mind, but awareness itself. That which sees itself is awareness. It's essentially not what we're aware of – it's that which is aware.

The whole universe – all worlds and all objects – appear both upon and in awareness. When awareness then identifies with those objects, the sense of individuality, the "I am", is born and with it separation and suffering. At some point, awareness realizes its mistake and remembers its true nature.

You aren't actually a someone, a person, who is conscious. You are the awake space of awareness itself, within which all the "thought up" entities in your world appear. Out of all these imagined entities, you have simply made the mistake of thinking that one of them is you.

*   *   *

Is there a difference between awareness and consciousness? And how does awareness, consciousness and the body–mind relate to one another?

Awareness is timeless and eternal, and this gives birth to consciousness. Consciousness is the background for the appearance of the body–mind.

At the core of the mind is consciousness and at the core of consciousness is the pure, non-dual, non-conceptual Absolute. Consciousness manifests out of the un-manifested dark radiance of pure awareness, the pure potentiality of the Absolute.

Awareness is that which perceives what the consciousness is doing as well as its comings and goings.

Consciousness is just a ripple, a wave rising and falling as a vibration or pulsation of presence/awareness. In that ripple, worlds, beings and all forms, including the body–mind you believe yourself to be, appear and disappear endlessly.

The death of the body causes the consciousness to return back to the source, which is the awareness itself. But this is just an appearance. What constitutes you never changes in birth or in death. You are always the primordial presence/awareness in which everything, including consciousness, comes and goes.

When you first start to inquire as to your true nature, you might begin to see that you are not the body–mind. Then you might identify yourself as the consciousness or witness that perceives everything. But then from that vantage point you begin to realize that this consciousness is just your universal body, the body of the Absolute, and that your ultimate nature is actually before consciousness.

* * *

**I am still under the impression that awareness comes
from the individual body–mind. I know when I am
hungry, but I do not know about any other body.
I can recognize my own thoughts; however, I cannot
recognize others' thoughts. If everything is one being,
shouldn't awareness know of what is happening to
other people and their minds and bodies?**

It does. There is only one awareness. It's the same as when
you are dreaming; there is only a single awareness that
brightens and encompasses everything you are dreaming
about.

Why do we, as this body–mind unit, not know what
is happening to other body–mind units? Because the one
asking the question, the "relative subject", is situated in
space and time. You could just as easily be wondering
why you are unable to know the beliefs, emotions and
experiences of the other people appearing in your dream.
The answer is that as the dream subject, you are playing
a limited part in the dream. A part cannot know the
whole dream, but the awareness containing the dream
is aware of the entire plot. This is why as you awaken
in the morning, you are able to know and interpret the
thoughts and intentions of each dream character.

Awareness is the only true One that experiences life, whether that life is the human, animal, plant or mineral form. Awareness is experiencing itself from infinite viewpoints and one of those viewpoints is through your body–mind.

You are the eyes, ears and senses of the Absolute.

3

SIMPLE ORDINARY AWARENESS

"ENLIGHTENMENT IS NOT ABOUT BECOMING DIVINE.
INSTEAD IT'S ABOUT BECOMING MORE FULLY HUMAN."
— LAMA SURYA DAS

One morning, the master made an announcement that one of his monks had achieved an advanced state of enlightenment. Of course the other monks were very excited over the news. A few of them wanted to see this young man for themselves and so went to visit him. "We heard you are enlightened," they said. "How do you feel?" "As miserable as ever," replied the monk.

The point of this story is that even after awakening, you're still you! You will not go through a miraculous change and have a complete transformation of your personality. Individuals that are normally sullen do not start running around smiling and laughing all the time.

Neither does enlightenment mean that you won't ever have troubles again. You will still need to work, keep your job and pay your bills. You will still have car problems and your children will get the flu. You could still be passed up for that promotion at work and your partner may forget your birthday.

Your friends will not look at you and say, "You look different today. Were you enlightened over the weekend?" Others will not necessarily recognize you as a special person, especially if they are your family and friends.

You don't become a special, higher being. In fact, it's the opposite. You realize you are the same as everybody and everything else.

Outwardly, you may not change at all and you will probably continue playing the roles you had before, but with one main difference; awareness is the one playing those roles and you see that this has always been so! You've just been thinking you were in charge.

THE MYTH OF PERSONAL ENLIGHTENMENT

In all the stories about enlightenment, there comes a point where something happens and in an instant the monk is deeply enlightened. From that point on we imagine the "happily ever after" monk serenely floating around on a cloud of bliss.

The reality is that even the most awakened teachers on the planet today still live in the world, raise families, get sick and run out of milk.

Awakening doesn't make all your problems disappear and it is not like a beautiful painting that you can acquire and hang on your wall to admire.

The initial experience of awakening, like falling in love, can be blissful, ecstatic and even transcendent. But the day-to-day experience of enlightenment, like marriage, is more like everyday life, where there are sunny days and there are windy and stormy ones.

WHAT DOES AWAKENING LOOK LIKE?

Adi Shankara, the famous Indian sannyasin (wandering ascetic), claimed that somebody who is enlightened would show no obvious sign or mark of a holy man. He also went on to say that the enlightened one could appear as a wise man or as a fool. He can seem feeble of mind or be a king. He can be quiet and relaxed or he can be a leader of men. He may be insulted by all or honoured by all. He may even be ignored.

Arthur Osborne, who chronicled the life of India's renowned sage Ramana Maharshi, spent a long time in the Ramana ashram and wrote many books about Ramana. In one of those books, he claimed that even those who are completely awakened may not be noticeable in the slightest, and that Ramana himself was not seen as awakened until he started to share his knowledge with others and they began to look to him as a guru.

Someone who is awake may not say, "I have awakened." They may not claim anything at all, because when somebody is truly enlightened, they no longer believe in the concept of a separate "I". They know that what they are is no-thing. This is not a total absence of anything at all but a no-thing that is full of everything. When this no-thing recognizes itself, this is what is sometimes called awakening.

THE ENLIGHTENED EGO

The ego is the one that wants to get enlightened, so it can walk around gloating and feeling good about itself for having "arrived". But the joke is on us. The ego is not going to be there at that moment. There will be no one there to enjoy possessing it.

This is the last trick in the ego's arsenal of subtle delusion. This is what is called the "enlightened ego".

The enlightened ego likes to read and memorize all the spiritual scriptures it can lay its hands on. It will use all this knowledge to frame eloquent arguments with such philosophical acumen as to show everybody else how enlightened it is. If people around expect an enlightened person to wear robes, the enlightened ego will wear robes (unwrinkled, of course). Or it will move to a foreign country or wear the appropriate beatific smile on its face. It will even live life in service to the sick and the impoverished if that is going to complete the illusion of having attained enlightenment.

Belief in a personal enlightenment is the ultimate trick that the ego will play on itself.

NOTICING WHAT IS ALREADY PRESENT

The following questions are meant to help point you to the realization of what is present right now, yet perhaps not fully recognized or appreciated.

As you consider each question, be honest about your actual experience and not what you think you already know. As you begin to sink deeper within the questions, you will start to get glimpses of your essential self that are founded on your direct experience, not on your ideas.

1. Are you present and aware right now, in this very moment? Can you see that you are completely here and aware of being here?

2. Noticing that you are actually here, present and aware, does this require any thinking?

3. Can you see that thoughts, emotions, feelings and sensations are coming and going in this space of pure aware intelligence?

4. Can you also see that all objects, events and experiences are happening in this intelligent space?

Perhaps in the attempt to answer these questions, you began to become aware of a silent, obvious, clear, present awareness, a consciousness that has the capacity to recognize itself.

As you look even deeper into this silent pristine awareness, notice that every thought, feeling, sensation and experience comes and goes in this clear natural knowingness that knows all these appearances, in this moment, and then this moment, and then this moment.

In truth, has this aware presence ever shifted or changed in the face of any situation? Is it necessary to wait for a future event for the recognition that you are this aware presence, right now?

THERE IS ONLY BEING

There is no separate entity that could be enlightened or unenlightened. There are only innumerable expressions of the One Being (which we call people, animals, forms), mirror-like facets, reflecting beingness back to itself.

Enlightenment is "seeing" this truth but with no "seer" and no "seen". In enlightenment, the seer and the seen merge and arise together in the space of ever-present awareness as the expression and vehicle for Spirit, the eyes, ears and body of the Absolute, seeing all manifested reality as a ripple of Itself.

You, the one reading these words now, are not separate from the one who wrote them. We are the same. The only difference between you and me lies in the ever-changing perceived, not the never-changing perceiver. That perceiver is only One. The One that experiences itself as your body–mind is the same One that experiences itself in every other body–mind, form or appearance that exists.

IT'S THE OCEAN THAT REALIZES ITSELF IN YOU

You are the ocean, yet you have believed yourself to be just one of its waves. As a wave, yes you are limited. You are born and you will suffer death, crashing against the shore, never to be seen again. We call these waves "consciousness" and they contain your entire life story and yet they are limited expressions of what you are. The reality is that you are actually the ocean itself, the very source of all waves. When the wave is no longer interesting, there is the opportunity to step back and notice your infinite presence as the ocean.

As long as you take yourself to be something contained within the temporary, you will never know the limitlessness that you are. In truth, you are never limited. Just as the ocean taking itself to be a wave does not actually divide the ocean into parts, so taking yourself to be a limited entity does not limit the totality that you are.

Realization is not about you, the wave, realizing it is the ocean. The ocean realizes itself in you and reveals itself to have never been just a wave. Nothing changes except the falling away of a false belief.

*   *   *

I have been meditating for many years, but apart from some wonderful but fleeting experiences, the final revelation of my true nature hasn't happened yet ...

What do you think is going to happen? Awareness is normally so ordinary and simple that it's easily missed.

If you expect something more dramatic, you may not recognize what is already here. Or if you do recognize it, you may not be happy with it because you want more fireworks than you are getting. Thunderbolts that wipe away all your conditioning, a storm zapping your mind clean.

Your original state is much more simple, gentle and ordinary. It sneaks up on you from behind as the spacious awareness that hosts everything including the sense of self that wants something more than this utter simplicity.

You don't have to see fireworks, there will be no special audience with God and you will not be lifted into the sky by hosts of angels. It will be just you, the same as before. I'm sorry to fizzle out all your mind's projections of what will happen when this special state visits you, but this is just the plain truth.

Spiritual experiences and lights shooting out of your third eye are in the end just spiritual entertainment and they will dry out and fade faster than a thousand-petal lotus.

Even amazing states of bliss, peace, clarity and spaciousness have nothing to do with awakening as these are just experiences coming and going in the impersonal awareness that you are. Some of these experiences may last a long time, giving the impression that this is the real thing, but they will eventually always change when you stop the practices that lead you to them. However, you as you truly are remains always as the unshakable presence in which all experiences appear and disappear.

"Looking forward" to what you think enlightenment might be at some grand point in the future keeps you from seeing the truth of its presence right now. You are aware in this moment, aren't you? You are already here, so keep your focus here.

If you stay with this spacious and alert awakeness, you will realize that there is only one thing, one player, one presence, and that is always already enlightened.

*   *   *

So, you're telling me that I have spent years looking for something that I had all along? That I will end up at the same point at which I started? That there is no more to it than that? That makes no sense!

The short answer is "yes". It's that simple. You have always been what you were looking for. You don't move toward the truth of what you are; you start from there.

We realize that there is nothing out there that we need to find to complete ourselves. Everything is One, this One is all that there is and we are included in this One.

Your questions are perhaps more profound than you realize. Just the simple act of asking the questions you asked is an indication that you are beginning to see the truth.

Stop thinking that you need to find something to become something. All you are looking for is awareness. And you are already aware. It is your aware self that is reading this page.

*   *   *

What has changed for you since your realization?

What has changed? What is different now? Absolutely nothing. I didn't attain special powers or special insights, and I didn't really come closer to my true nature. It just seems that I lost some ideas and beliefs about what I was. The truth is nothing really happened because I have always been what I am, even when I was identified as a separate identity and a spiritual seeker.

The only difference now is that I don't perceive that there is anything wrong, including getting caught up in the entity because I know I am not that entity. Before, it was definitely not okay. The quest was always for perfection, always for something different. In the realization that It is already here and everything is It , you lose your spiritual self-importance that makes you want to attain something better, something higher, something holier than this.

So what has changed? Absolutely nothing. Just seeing life as it is, as it always was, and always will be. Not my life, but simply life itself.

PRESENCE PAUSE

LOOKING NAKEDLY, RESTING STILL

If you just look around right now you will notice many objects, but did you notice the space in which the objects appear? Only a very few people will notice the space in which those objects are contained. But as soon as they are made aware of it, everyone can see that space. Recognizing who you are, your real Self, can be viewed in a similar way. Your body–mind, the mind-made entity you believe yourself to be, is an object in awareness just as is a tree or a cloud that arises in the space.

Look directly into this aware intelligence that allows you to notice the space around you. Take a moment, this moment, and notice this awakeness that is looking through your eyes right now. You can get a sense of this by first simply looking out through your eyes and then "looking back" at that which is doing the looking.

Can you sense this centre of awareness behind the eyes? Where is it located? Is it within your eyes or a space in your head? Does it have a shape or a colour or an actual centre? Does it have any borders? Does this aware space have any sense of self or identity apart from thoughts, feelings and sensations floating by? Is this awareness nothingness or is it brightly awake?

Notice what this wakefulness is and rest in it as long as you can.

PART 2

PRACTICE OR NO PRACTICE, AND WHICH PRACTICE?

"GOD DWELLS IN YOU, AS YOU, AND YOU DON'T HAVE TO
'DO' ANYTHING TO BE GOD-REALIZED OR SELF-REALIZED;
IT IS ALREADY YOUR TRUE AND NATURAL STATE. JUST
DROP ALL SEEKING, TURN YOUR ATTENTION INWARD, AND
SACRIFICE YOUR MIND TO THE ONE SELF RADIATING IN
THE HEART OF YOUR VERY BEING."
– RAMANA MAHARSHI

When it comes to awakening and the debate over practice or no practice, there are many different schools of thought.

One camp feels that awakening is something that just happens and that any practice reinforces the illusion of a separate entity that needs to strive to achieve a goal.

The other camp believes that awakening is something you have to work for and that practice is absolutely necessary to free oneself from the grasp of the ego/mind.

Who is right? The answer is both and neither.

While it is true that you are already what you seek, this is not the state of awareness that most human beings experience on a daily basis. Most people's awareness is in a state that does not include the totality of everything around them. We cling to things, clinging to seeing things as separate from ourselves. Our minds create an illusion that there is something out there that is lost and must be found in order for us to be complete. If this is where we are, we need to begin from here.

While it's true that we are always this presence, this vast spacious intelligence containing everything, unless this has been directly realized, this is not the experience of those of us still standing outside the "Gateless Gate".

There is nothing to do and nothing to get, yet we need to start from where we are.

4

TRUTH IS THAT
WHICH KNOWS THE WAY

"LET YOURSELF BE SILENTLY DRAWN
BY THE STRANGE PULL OF WHAT YOU REALLY LOVE.
IT WILL NOT LEAD YOU ASTRAY."
– RUMI

To know how to get somewhere, you first need to know where you are going. So to understand if practice is right for you or not, you need to be clear about what you are seeking.

If your aim is simply to be your true nature, no practice is needed for that. If it is really your nature, truly what you already are, then you can neither achieve it nor escape it. It is not something you can attain, nor something you can cast off. It is inevitably what you are, right now. It requires no action on your part. You cannot encounter it. You cannot do it. You cannot help but be it. Though you cannot see it, it is with you, as you. What is the need to "practice" if the goal is already here?

If your goal is more tangible or practical, be it something like, "I know that I am awareness, but I want to ... silence the mind, release the questions, live in bliss, work through my psychological pain, achieve extraordinary powers ..." and so on, then accomplishing this goal will be in the realm of experience rather than the realm of simply being what you already are. To achieve your phenomenal goal, whatever it may be, what is required is a phenomenal solution, a "practice".

NO GATES IN THIS ONE MOMENT

The Buddha's highest most profound teaching was a direct pointing to our true nature, awareness itself. But as some people didn't understand this view, Buddha gave out various relative teachings and practices. Why? To address the conceptual positions that these people imagined themselves to be in.

Ramana Maharshi stated, "You are awareness; awareness is another name for you. Since you are awareness, there is no need to attain or cultivate it." But he also recognized that not everyone could realize this truth instantly, and so he prescribed different practices according to the maturity of the seeker.

HOW DO YOU DECIDE WHICH WAY IS BETTER FOR YOU?

The renowned Indian sage Nisargadatta Maharaj said, "You must find your own way. Unless you find it yourself, it will not be your own way and it will take you nowhere."

At the level of absolute truth we are already enlightened, free and complete. At the level of relative truth we experience suffering because we haven't yet realized this.

Both truths apply. They are inseparable, two sides of one coin, and the goal is not to pick one or the other but to embrace both. There are pros and cons with either the direct path or the path that progresses.

THE PROGRESSIVE PATH

The path that progresses is comforting to the mind. It gives a sense of belonging and the intense practices can still the mind and its unruly thoughts. However, a progressing path can also undermine the possibility of direct, immediate awakening by reinforcing the belief that your true nature is not here and now and that awakening requires time and effort.

It's possible that a prolonged, gradual practice can strengthen the ego by solidifying the image of the spiritual seeker. Once this seeker identity is firmly entrenched, it becomes difficult to clearly see and release that identity because the identified seeker is striving for a dualistic experience based on an "I/me" that is separate from the truth it seeks. This identified seeker becomes firmly entrenched and will eventually manifest an experience for itself that is mistaken for enlightenment.

I am not suggesting that all spiritual practices should be discarded. Not at all. The problem is not with the practice but how it is practised, meaning if it is goal-oriented. If your practice is bound to a goal, this is an obstacle because there is no goal to be achieved. What you are looking for is here now and has always been. When the mind is freed from any desire to "become", the attention that has been projected outward toward something shifts spontaneously from the object it is seeking to the perceiver of the object, which is a taste of one's own true self.

THE DIRECT PATH

The direct path, on the other hand, while it provides the opportunity to discover our true nature here and now, can also lead us astray if we mistaken intellectual knowledge for realization. Simply understanding that we are awareness is just the first step. To leave it as a mental theory is not going to help much. Our original nature is not something we "imagine"; it is originally and naturally so, and this must be directly realized.

Awakening is a direct realization of our true nature. It is not an intellectual knowledge or even an experience. While it's true that "we are always the Self", if this hasn't been truly and directly realized, this knowledge won't do us any good. Just knowing that there is no gate to pass through doesn't mean that we are at the end of the search, not if we are still standing outside that gateless gate.

THE ULTIMATE TRUTH IS A PATHLESS PATH

If we are truly honest with ourselves, we can discover what approach we really need and at what time.

If our mind is restless with a million thoughts, we may need a bit of discipline to bring it under control, in which case a short meditation on the breath, on a candle, on the face of our guru, etc may help. After the mind has calmed down, we can move to a more contemplative state, to the practice-less practice of noticing what is already here, the presence that has never left and is our essential nature.

On the other hand, if our mind becomes too uptight, dry, rigid and controlling of its experience, it's time to forget about practices for a while and go spend a few days down at the beach or up in the mountains to loosen up a bit.

If practice is happening in this moment, then it is apparent this is what we need until we no longer need it. The same realization that we achieved through practice may present itself to someone else while they are raising a child, or driving down the road, or sitting in a prison cell. All paths are valid, but in the end we find that the realization of the ultimate truth is a pathless path.

KEEP THE MIND FREE

Contemplate the following, and if you wish, write your answers down in your journal of self-inquiry.

- Do I need a practice?
- What is the purpose of my practice?
- What am I hoping to get from a practice?

Then do what you must and relinquish all thoughts about it. The thought, "I must practise/not practise to get enlightened" is as much a distraction as any other thoughts that float by in the mind. Let that thought go. Keep your mind free.

The bottom line is that all the different viewpoints, "meditate, don't meditate; you are nothing, you are God on Earth", are all relative viewpoints, a matter of conditioning and cultural trapping.

If someone believes that they have the monopoly on the truth, they lack clarity and insight. Nothing can be the total truth in the worlds of manifestation and the more solid our concepts, the more likely they are going to sink us, sooner or later.

True realization is a full un-grasping of any perspective and the ability to see all perspectives at the same time. The mind can never open like this if it is clinging to one perspective. Only awareness, our true complete natural state, can reveal this.

If people say that no practice is needed to awaken, awareness sees the truth in that. If people say that you need a practice to awaken, awareness also sees the truth in that.

To see truth in all beliefs, without having to believe in any of it, is true freedom.

* * *

If there's nothing "I" can do in order to become awake, then why should I try so hard at my meditation practice?

The concept that there is "nothing I can do" is a waste of time. I don't agree that there is nothing you can do. Here's something you can do: look inside yourself and try to find this elusive someone you refer to with the pronouns "I" and "me". If you disregard all past memories you have of yourself, is this "I" or "me" anywhere to be found? Is there in fact anything concrete to be found?

If you truly look, you will not find a separate "I" no matter how long or hard you search. This is because it simply does not exist. However, this cannot be just an intellectual understanding. You have to see this, to experience this, for yourself.

In the words of Ramana Maharshi, it is no different from thinking you see a snake on the road, yet upon closer examination you find that it is simply a rope. It was never a snake; you only thought it was.

Only when you search for an individual "I" and do not succeed in locating it will you understand that awareness is what you are and, in that, you will discover your true identity.

At first, you might feel vulnerable at this no-seeing. You might think that it can't be right and so you will quickly go back to searching for your identity or trying to figure out what you are doing wrong. This is where you must return to the no-seeing and begin to trust in this no-seeing.

Eventually you begin to feel comfortable and relaxed in this, realizing that you are not a thing, not a person called "I" or "me". You realize that what you truly are is only this aware presence – awareness aware of itself as awareness.

*   *   *

In your experience, what is the simplest, most direct and effective practice for waking up and staying awake?

If you had lost yourself, how far would you need to go to find yourself? All that would be needed is to remember that you are you, and you are right here, right now. How much training is needed for that?

Just be aware of the sense of awakeness that is always here. Now, don't think about what you have just read. Simply notice the awakeness that is seeing the world through your eyes now and is always seeing the world through your eyes. Are you aware right now? Are you really separate from the awareness, even now?

This seeing is timeless and never leaves you or changes. This is simply what your nature is. It is just that simple. Return to this still point whenever you are overtaken by mental clutter. The answer to any question is to go back to this still point that you are.

*   *   *

Are you still practising and do you think there are deeper layers of awareness for you to realize?

Yes, sometimes I practise but I don't do it to deepen into this. And I truly cannot say if there is more than this.

On one hand, when you realize the truth of the situation, you realize the totality of it. So from this point of view there is no deepening. On the other hand, there may be infinite possibilities of being here now, a continuous evolving into this, a continuous deepening into this, where truth reveals itself more and more with the apparent passage of time and space.

In this moment, and this moment, and this moment, it is complete and there is nothing further I need to get, understand or know.

5

REAL MEDITATION IS LETTING GO OF CONTROL

"CEASE PRACTICE BASED ON INTELLECTUAL
UNDERSTANDING, PURSUING WORDS AND FOLLOWING
AFTER SPEECH. LEARN THE BACKWARD STEP THAT
TURNS YOUR LIGHT INWARD TO ILLUMINATE WITHIN.
BODY AND MIND OF THEMSELVES WILL DROP AWAY AND
YOUR ORIGINAL FACE WILL BE MANIFEST."
– DŌGEN

Most people, when they sit and meditate, try to guide and control their experience. They try to have fewer thoughts and achieve more peace so that the "I" they believe themselves to be can feel better. Of course the mind may become quieter, for a while anyway, and you might feel better, more peaceful, but sooner or later the mind will have something to say about being forced to shut up.

When meditation becomes a "means to an end", we get stuck. In its struggle to remain in control, the mind will learn the various techniques to quiet itself, to become more mindful, to achieve stillness, insight, peace, and it will fool us into thinking we are progressing. But these are just mental states that have nothing to do with the true, unfabricated peace and stillness of your true nature, which cannot be achieved but only revealed.

If you teach the mind how to stay quiet, after some effort it will do so and may even get so good at it that you will think you have reached the ultimate, effortless state. But if your practice fabricates an enlightened state in which everything is peaceful and clear because there are no thoughts, that state is the result of mental effort.

The attention has been trained to not follow the movement of thought, to abide in itself without really knowing itself. And because this state is the product of the mind, it will eventually wear off. It may take years, but the minute you stop the practice, it will start to fade away.

FALL INTO THE AWARE PRESENCE THAT CONTAINS IT ALL

The awakened state is the natural state of being. Natural means effortless, spontaneous, not contrived, not edited by anything. We can't arrive at a natural stateless state with the manipulation or application of a technique.

People feel that if they let go of control, nothing will happen but awakening is slipping behind the meditator, behind the one engaged in the doing and the mastering. *Awakening arises through the mind, not from the mind.*

When we let go of control and accept what our experience actually is, we disengage the meditator, the controller, the manipulator, and the one applying effort. Then we can investigate what happens when we actually let go of control. This is not "doing nothing" or being lazy. It is applying just enough effort to be alert and aware, and enough surrender or relaxation to release the grasp of the mind.

The stories that we tell ourselves are the creation of a separate meditator. The two most prominent stories being "I need to meditate to become enlightened," or "I've already got it and I don't need to meditate." All along it is our belief in these stories that keeps us separate from the true self.

All stories rise and fall like waves on the ocean of the Self. We don't need to indulge them or get rid of them.

Whether we decide to meditate or not, fall into the aware presence that contains it all.

ALWAYS ALREADY HERE

Our true nature is not produced nor is it created; it is always already here. In the same way that the sun is always present even when obscured by clouds, our true nature is obscured by patterns of body and mind that we mistake for ourselves.

Zen Master Eihei Dōgen said, "The Tao is basically perfect and all-pervading. How could it depend on practice and realization?" In other words, your essential self is already here and doesn't depend on realization and practice. Yet as long as your mind is confused by concepts and beliefs, Dōgen also advised his students "to take the backward step that turns your light inward to illuminate the self."

What keeps us from realizing our already present true nature is the desire to have things, do things and accumulate things all for the "I" we think we are. This drags our attention out into the "becoming", because when we are attentive to "something" we are fixated on that something.

If we reverse the flow of attention to attention itself, we are free from all grasping. By resting in this shining, clear, peaceful, unassuming, steady, solid awareness, we know it to be the truth of our being.

HOW DOES ONE REVERSE "CAUGHT" ATTENTION?

By placing the attention on the one paying attention. *By paying attention to what is paying attention.*

What is the difference between paying attention and thinking? These are two very different things. They happen independently of one another. Paying attention is an experience; thinking is a construction. Simply experience that which is paying attention and rest in that.

The attention then shifts to perception itself, the awareness in which everything appears and disappears. This step is the "backward step" that Dōgen spoke of and what I call Instant Presence.

This "practice" is not about getting something you don't have, but about recognizing what you already are. There is no need to try to attain what you actually are. Natural aware presence is not something you do, it's not something you attain, because it is already self-existing. If it resonates with you, it can be used as a means of support in your recognition of what is always naturally present.

*   *   *

**I study with a spiritual teacher and I have been
practising with him for a few years. His advice is to
keep the attention as much as possible on awareness by
asking yourself, every time you are distracted, "What
am I giving my attention to?"**

Becoming conscious of where our attention is focused is
a spiritual practice that helps to cut the identification with
the mind. Eventually, however, we must realize that even
attention itself is a phenomenon that must be abandoned.
Even the attention, our most potent instrument of
perception, is merely another fiction.

What is it that is aware of attention? What is aware of
its presence or absence? There is something behind and
before the attention that is even simpler, more subtle,
and that exists without effort. What is this?

These are the questions that you need to ask yourself.
The words are pointing to something. What are they
pointing to?

This is where we must do away with answers –
intellectual, mental or verbal. Here only direct realization
will do.

Regardless of what techniques or methods you use,
create some time where you let go of all "doings" and

simply rest in Natural Presence, simply letting everything be just as it is.

Discover who you are when you let life be just what it is.

Discover what happens when there is no one controlling or making an effort at all, when you simply let everything be just as it is. Discover who you are when there is no managing of life just as it is.

*   *   *

For four years I have practised Ramana Maharshi's method of self-inquiry, asking myself "Who Am I?" However, I am still unable to receive an intuitive sense of who I really am.

The teachings of Ramana Maharshi, one of the greatest sages of the last century, are the teachings of self-inquiry through the question, "Who am I?"

The answer to "Who am I?" is irrelevant. What's relevant is the looking.

Asking the question, "Who am I?" is like holding up a mirror to try to look at yourself, yet no matter how much you look, nothing appears in the mirror. The "I" can never be found. But, at the same time, you are here. Look at that sense of "am-ness", the sense of existing, here and now.

When you ask yourself the question "Who am I?" you will immediately notice a vast space, and that vast space is the answer. Ask the question, and then stop there, at the edge of a vast aware space of not knowing. Go no further. Allow the answer to reveal itself.

The point is not to find an answer. If you find an answer, throw it away. Any answer you find is useless.

*   *   *

During meditation I sometimes enter a space that feels very still and peaceful but I quickly lose consciousness and I come out feeling vague and spacey ...

There is an experience that can sometimes happen during meditation where the awareness aspect of our original nature has been left out and consciousness is frozen in a kind of blank spaciness.

Some people think that this is our original nature, but it is not.

Remaining in an open but vacant state is to be blocked off from everything – no thoughts, no emotions and no awareness either. We may as well be a corpse. There may be no thoughts, we may feel empty, but the perceiving capacity is blocked off, frozen within a vacant state.

Because the wakefulness aspect is missing, this is nothing but a mind state of nothingness. All that one is doing in this still, vacant state is not following thoughts, but at the same time one is grasping or being fixated on stillness. The focus of attention is within itself, but it still doesn't know itself. There is still an observer (consciousness) and an observed (stillness).

Being truly free is going beyond both the observed and the observer.

When you watch anything, there is always the observer and the thing being observed, but that observer is not a separate entity – that observer is the product of thought. There is no difference between the two.

When what is observed is realized as being the same as the observer, duality, conflict and the self comes to an end and it is realized that the emptiness or openness that is left is the true nature of the observer.

When you rest in awareness, every object is its own subject – we are not looking at stillness or peace or a flower; we are the stillness, the peace and the flower.

The observer is not a separate subject looking at an object, but it arises with the observed in the space of ever-present awareness as the expression and vehicle for Spirit, the eyes, ears and body of the Absolute, seeing the manifested reality as the Absolute sees it: everything, including the observer, as a ripple in the Awareness that I Am.

Keep looking directly into this, remembering that anything you can see is an object appearing in what you are. Keep discarding object after object, including the concept of nothingness. Something remains. What is that?

6

ALLOWING NATURAL MEDITATION TO HAPPEN

"TO REALIZE THE INEXPRESSIBLE TRUTH, DO NOT MANIPULATE MIND OR BODY BUT SIMPLY OPEN INTO TRANSPARENCY WITH RELAXED, NATURAL GRACE."
– TILOPA

In our day-to-day life, we are almost always habitually involved with thoughts and projections, constantly trying to manipulate whatever comes up in our life experiences by either moving toward the ones we like or moving away from the ones we don't.

The thoughts themselves are not the problem. The problem is that we are constantly reacting to them and so every thought that arises in the mind continually distracts us, seemingly obscuring our true nature –natural awareness. By natural awareness here I refer to our true naked nature, stripped bare of these movements of the mind. Since the mind depends on this constant movement for its continued existence, the practice of *Instant Presence* is to be internally still and undistracted. This means leaving everything that arises in our experience (thoughts, sights, sounds and sensations) as it is, without manipulations or strategies. We simply relax in the present moment without trying to improve it, correct it or replace it.

This is not a passive surrender but a letting go to being totally present and totally relaxed at the same time, without any artificiality or manipulation. Instead of our usual habit of grasping and making the moment solid, we open, dissolve and "let everything be".

Essentially, this is the complete practice. There is nothing else that we are doing.

STOP ALL MOVEMENT AND LET SPONTANEOUS PRESENCE BE

The practice of Instant Presence is an opening, a relaxing of our focus (while maintaining alertness) and letting everything come to us instead of us chasing after something (even though the reality is that awareness doesn't "come" to us because we already are that).

The words "relaxing into it while maintaining alertness" seem to point to a mind-made effort, but what I'm talking about is to leave the mind as it is, without giving it anything to do.

We don't need to withdraw from the world and go deep into ourselves to reach some "advanced state". This only obstructs the free flow of our natural state and conditions us to believe that our already enlightened nature is somewhere other than right where we are, as we are, right now.

Instead, we just trust, connect and realize what is already here.

LUMINOUS COGNIZING EMPTINESS

The practice of Instant Presence is simply to remain undistracted from present wakefulness, to relax and open in all directions, without spacing out and losing our alertness. To be as open and relaxed as possible while being present and lucid with all our senses wide open. This is the marriage between emptiness, spaciousness (the female aspect of awareness) and the knowingness or cognizing aspect (the male part).

Straying too far into the empty aspect of our true nature makes us spaced out, ungrounded and foggy. Relaxed awareness is neither spacey nor hazy. It needs to be alert and vivid, not like a drug-induced state or a dream. If we move too far in that direction we start losing interest in everything. On the other hand, when we stray too far into the knowingness aspect, we become uptight and controlling of our experience, we forget the emptiness aspect of our nature and we become caught up in the world.

How can we find the right balance between the two? First, if possible, give up all effort and rest in the total effortlessness of this awareness now. If distractions happen, use the minimum of "effort" necessary to be clear and awake while letting things be, without trying to change or modify them.

Once the light of awareness is switched on, remember to let go of the switch and return to formless awareness or you will just keep switching the light on and off. Just let go of the switch and the one switching it on and off.

Rest in what is, this moment – just accept it and be in harmony with the moment as it is.

THE PRACTICE OF INSTANT PRESENCE IN A NUTSHELL

In this practice we simply rest in a natural, effortless way without manipulations or strategies.

We take a break from making anything happen or not happen. We are not trying to be anything or anyone, nor attempting to change or accomplish anything. We are just resting in what is happening moment by moment.

We rest directly in the spontaneity of our natural, unadulterated being, without fabricating, rejecting or changing anything.

Effortlessly, without thinking or trying to figure anything out, we allow everything that arises in our experience (thoughts, sights, sounds and sensations) to be as it is.

We don't choose the thoughts, feelings or experiences that come into awareness but rather meet them when they do, without judgement.

We rest in silence, as the silence. This silence is beginningless and endless and our body and the world are here in this spacious awareness, permeated with the sound of vibrant silence.

We simply rest as awareness, aware of itself.

*   *   *

Since awareness is not an object, I realize it is impossible for me to focus on it. Therefore, what might help me is to steer my attention away from sensations and thoughts. Am I correct in moving in this direction?

Indeed you are. You are definitely on the right track; however, you cannot use your will to steer your attention away from your thoughts. The reason is because this in itself is a thought. Instead, just notice what is going on.

When you attempt to focus by "un-focusing", you are operating at the level of the mind. Doing this will not really help you recognize awareness. This "practice" of resting in awareness is not a training to get rid of thought; it is being free of involvement with thoughts.

Awareness is the formless, timeless and eternal space within which all the thoughts you have about it and all of the practices you perform in an attempt to attain it, have their existence.

* * *

**Where do I keep my focus during the practice of
Instance Presence?**

We do not focus inwardly, outwardly or anywhere in-between. We stop all movement toward anything and let spontaneous presence just be. This frees us from the witness and the witnessed, the doer and the deed and what is left is the true nature of both.

* * *

**Must we surrender our ego to truly experience
the truth of our real nature? And, if so, what
does that involve?**

Ego just means the identification with a separate entity. Awareness is what we are. Ego is what we believe we are. Once the recognition that who we are as this all-pervading awareness has occurred, the notion that the ego is separate from awareness begins to dissolve. Then the ego is seen not as an enemy, but simply as an aspect of the Source and it is realized that there is only That, the Absolute, the One without a second, unfolding in the shape and form of the ordinary. The classic example is the ocean and its many expressions as wave, foam or spray. Regardless of the form the water takes, it is still ocean. The source that is functioning through the saint and the sinner, the drug addict and the monk, the psychopath and the guru, is the same. Sometimes the expression of that source is ugly, sometimes beautiful, sometimes tragic and sometimes blissful.

The real meaning of ego surrender is to surrender to our true nature, to relax and release the ego's hold on what it thinks is reality and realize that our true nature is the totality of being.

How? By forgetting everything we know about the ego and who we believe we are and shift our attention totally to the beingness, the alertness that is reading these words right now. Dive deep into the place where you gained the ego and lost yourself.

Where is the ego now?

PRESENCE PAUSE

THE GATELESS GATE

Set aside 15–20 minutes to sit comfortably, lie down if you can, without falling asleep. The body should be relaxed and still. Keep your eyes open, but not wide open trying to see something. Just relaxed, soft, watery eyes, taking in your environment without being focused on anything in particular. The mouth is relaxed and the breath is natural and unforced. All the senses are wide open in all directions without trying to grasp anything. Your whole beingness should be left open and alert but not focused on anything in particular.

Soften your mental focus and open your consciousness up 360 degrees all around. Listen to the sounds around you. Open the ears in all directions, but without trying to nail any particular sound and without letting your attention move from sound to sound. Just stay relaxed and alert, while at the same time allowing listening to happen.

Allow other sensations in as well: the feeling of the weight of your body against the chair or the bed, your heart beating, a rumbling of the stomach. There may also be more subtle sensations like heat, pressure, energy, pain, pleasure. Don't focus on any particular sensation; just be aware of the multi-dimensional play of sensation within your whole body, including the head and face.

After several minutes allow your body's boundaries or edges to dissolve and inner sounds and sensations to merge with outer sounds and sensations. Allow your awareness to expand in all directions; front, back, sides, above and below. Cultivate the feeling of opening up absolutely, nakedly, to the entire universe.

Awareness is now aware of the full range of sounds and sensations both outside and inside the body. Relax even deeper into this spacious knowingness, just as it is, without trying to hold it, grasp it or understand it. Let it be what it is, not worried by ideas of how long it is going to last. Don't try to "see" anything or make anything happen. Don't force anything, don't chase thoughts; let everything be as it is. If you become too relaxed, you may space out or fall asleep. If you try too hard, if you concentrate too much, you may get uptight and stressed out. The right balance is 50/50. So if you start to feel spaced out, maybe get up or take a deep breath or adjust the way you are sitting to a more upright and alert position. Even move to a colder room or step outside. Sharpen the attention, the alertness.

If you feel yourself becoming "tight", take a deep relaxing breath, soften your face, your eyes, your body, your posture, and emphasize the relaxation aspect more. Now just rest here.

JUST REST IN THIS MOMENT

At first, we may only be able to rest in this aware presence for a few seconds before we are distracted by thoughts.

When thoughts arise, has the aware presence gone anywhere? Have you gone anywhere? No, your attention has just been caught in a thought. Why does this happen? Because you still believe that the thought says something about you. You still believe that there is an "I" who is the owner of the thought and that this "I" is you.

When this happens, refrain from judging your practice or your progress. Everything that arises is simply the play of awareness and everything is naturally perfect just as it is. Every time you get distracted, just simply bring the attention back toward awareness itself.

Relax into this aware presence many times throughout the day. If you try to sustain presence/awareness for long stretches, it can become a goal-oriented mental practice. So try to spend time as often as you can during the day just being still within this objectless, timeless, eternal and enduring space.

When we are able to truly penetrate this practice, what we thought we were dissolves into a space that is free of any concepts of self. At the same time we also experience a sharp lucidity without thought. These two aspects together are what is called presence or awareness, our original nature. Then we see nakedly, clearly and we realize that we have always been This.

PART 3

FLIP-FLOPPING – LOSING AND FINDING YOURSELF

"ONCE THE CLOUDS CLEAR, THE SKY FILLS WITH
SUNLIGHT, OUR TRUE NATURE SHINES THROUGH."
– DZOGCHEN PONLOP

When I was a child in primary school, as soon as our teacher, Mrs Lombardo, was out of the classroom my friends and I would start throwing pencils, erasers and rolled-up pieces of paper at each other.

Some of the boys decided that a piece of paper rolled in the mouth and well lubricated with spit would not only travel further but that it would also totally gross out the girls.

One of the boys' spit-balls suddenly hit my knee and got stuck there. He laughed.

"You didn't get me," I quickly replied. "You only got my knee." Then I aimed my rolled-up spit-ball at his face with a smash. For a second, the ball stuck to his cheek before dropping to the ground.

"You didn't get me either," he taunted, "you only got my face."

As kids we all knew that there was no place a spit-ball could hit that was actually "us". The same is true for our thoughts and emotions, which we continually identify as who we are.

BEING WHAT YOU CANNOT NOT BE

After we have had a glimpse, a taste, even a long drink of the truth, the experience of flip-flopping, seemingly finding and losing what we are, is a common experience. This experience can only ever be had by a separate entity; therefore, any reference to "finding/losing" awareness always takes for granted that a separate "me" actually exists in the first place.

As long as we still believe, however subtly, that we are limited to being a human being, we will experience this kind of back and forth "finding/losing". It just points to the fact that some belief in a separate self is still active.

UNFABRICATED ORIGINAL NATURE

Our original nature is composed of three qualities:

1. Unending sound or vibration (the sound of our original nature, the heavenly music spoken of in many mystical traditions).

2. Awareness or luminosity (the ability to perceive even without thought).

3. Sky-like vastness or emptiness (the container allowing for the arising and cognizing of everything).

Because we don't realize our nature, these three qualities become our voices, our thoughts and our physical bodies. As our attention flows to our words and the sounds we make, we forget our original sound. In like manner, our thoughts endlessly come and go, obscuring the unconditioned awareness aspect of our original nature. And as our attention flows out to the physical body, we forget our universal body of unlimited space.

In reality these qualities are present right now in body, speech and mind. However, we don't recognize them because our attention has shifted to the expression of the qualities rather than where the expression is coming from.

A CASE OF MISTAKEN IDENTITY

The vastness quality of our original nature allows everything to be in it, like the space in a room allows all objects in it to stay or to go. Without this spaciousness, also known as emptiness, nothing would be possible because this emptiness aspect of our being allows all things to be and all potentiality to manifest. It accommodates everything, including confusion and delusion and enlightenment. The spaciousness aspect of our essential nature gives the knowingness aspect absolute freedom to experience being lost and confused or enlightened and free.

The awareness aspect of our being is the same as the knowing aspect; the one that allows us to know that we are, that we exist. For example, when we notice a flower it is due to the knowingness aspect of our nature, while our spacious unconfined aspect, of emptiness, allows the flower to be there. No problem up to this point.

But if the knowingness forgets its emptiness aspect, it starts to believe that the flower is separate from itself. In this, the knowingness starts to believe that it is the subject, looking at the object that is the flower. This is the birth of the "I/me" entity and the start of delusion, because in reality this "I" is just another appearance, another object like the flower, appearing and disappearing in our original nature. All we need to do is reverse this flow and realize that we are and have always been what we are searching for. All that has happened is that the attention has moved out into form and identified with it. It's just a case of mistaken identity.

Understanding this is the first step, followed by returning the attention to the source of attention and re-stabilizing in it so that attention is not dragged out with every movement of the mind.

7

THE SEDUCTION OF THOUGHT

"ONE ENLIGHTENED THOUGHT AND ONE IS A BUDDHA,
ONE FOOLISH THOUGHT AND ONE IS AGAIN AN ORDINARY
PERSON. THAT IS WHAT WE HAVE TO PRACTISE WITH."
– HUINENG

Immediately after "my" realization, I confided what had happened to a spiritual friend who felt that I was conceited and possibly even deluded for talking about it. It's interesting how obsessed and inebriated we all can be by concepts of enlightenment and liberation until somebody close to us dares to suggest that they could actually have realized it. Then, scepticism, criticism and even anger can arise. This is simply the ego's defensive reaction against its own nothingness. In the end, everything is a reaction against that. It's scary for the ego to face its own non-existence.

While it may seem "rude" or "mean" for a friend to do that, it was really a blessing. In the past, what she said would have crushed me, it would have made me doubt, it would have thrown me into the mind – but it didn't. It didn't alter what had happened whatsoever, which showed me the depth of what was happening to me. It also revealed to me the mystery of flip-flopping, where a seeker, even one that has had a strong recognition of their true nature, can seemingly lose it once again. As I contemplated what my friend had said, there was an inner certainty that yes, "this is it". I also noticed that by trying to interpret, understand, analyse or explain this certainty, attention was turning automatically to the mind. Whenever that happens, we move away from direct experience back into concept, no longer connected to the certainty of spiritual perception. As soon as awareness saw this, attention once again collapsed in on itself, leaving no-thing.

HOW CAN YOU FIND SOMETHING THAT IS NOT LOST?

Most people unquestioningly assume that their thoughts are real, and as long as it is believed that they are real, we will turn toward them time and again. We turn to our minds to solve problems, all the while not realizing that it is the mind that creates the problems in the first place. The answers we are looking for will never be found in the mind.

Whenever our attention gets involved with thoughts it seems that awareness is obscured, but awareness is what is always here, doing the seeing. All that is happening when we think we've found it and then lost it, is that the focus of our attention has become fixated on some thought of a separate "I" entity that believes it can get it and lose it.

There is no such "I" in the picture whatsoever, apart from a thought that appears and disappears in the ever-present presence that we are.

Thoughts and beliefs of "finding/losing" are appearing and disappearing in the pristine presence of our true beingness. Once this is understood, it becomes easier to see clearly and the wavering back and forth ends once and for all.

PEACE, JOY AND CLARITY DO NOT COME AND GO

Notice that when the thought appears and disappears, it is appearing and disappearing in the naturally present, aware intelligence that contains and knows both the movement of thoughts and the stillness of no thoughts. Also notice that awareness doesn't appear when the thought appears and doesn't disappear when the thought leaves.

Peace, joy and clarity do not come and go. They are ever-present, flowing from our natural state; the presence/awareness that is always here. For this recognition, simply look away from the mind and see what is aware of the mind.

If you have the thought, "It has faded" or "I have lost it", who or what is aware of this thought? Investigate carefully the space in which everything appears. Can "this", your true nature, ever be lost? Notice that all that is happening is that you believe the thought, "It has faded." What has faded and what is still present even when the thought appears? Who or what is aware of this thought? See this. Investigate this.

The "you" that seems to "lose it and find it" is not who you actually are.

BE WHAT YOU ARE

Whatever you can possess and then lose is the content of awareness and not awareness itself. "Losing and finding" are the thoughts of this entity that you are identifying with and to which you have attributed an ongoing story, the story you consider your life. In this story, the entity, like in a dream, struggles with "losing and finding" the most elusive prize of all: enlightenment. But all of this is just a mind-created story.

Are you the entity in the story that is "getting closer", or are you the awareness in which the story appears?

Awareness is already constant. It's your thoughts, and your belief in those thoughts, that cause these apparent breaks in awareness. A break in awareness is simply a mental concept. What is it that is aware that there are breaks in awareness? Continue to be aware of that, and soon the breaks will be a thing of the past.

Continuous awareness occurs as a result of consistent surrender to it.

*   *   *

I am frequently distracted from awareness by thoughts.
How do I step out of thoughts?

The one who wants to step out of thought is itself another thought. A thought can never "step out" of itself. If ever you feel like you're succeeding in "stepping out", all that is happening is that the assumed "I" entity is giving itself a break from its own imaginary point of view.

Leave the thoughts alone. Don't touch them with another thought about them. Dismiss the story. It's just another distraction that keeps you focused in the wrong direction. It is the very thing that keeps you (seemingly) caught.

Be more interested in what your thoughts appear in and on. This is the direction to explore. Who watches the coming and going of thoughts? You, as the awareness, are fully present as the one knowing the thoughts. They appear in and on you.

When thoughts rush in, relax the focus a bit toward the awareness of the thoughts rather than the thoughts themselves. Understand that you are this awareness and not what is projected upon it.

When you no longer care whatever ephemeral thoughts and feelings arise, you stop empowering them by fighting them, resisting them, trying to control them or even watching them.

You are pure awareness and not what is projected upon it. Just be what you are. If you take the story, "I am full of thoughts, I am not there yet, there is still something missing" and discard it, what is left?

What is left is what you are.

Once the energy stops going to the thoughts, the show is over.

*   *   *

**Last year I experienced the unity of everything and
the knowing that I was connected with all that is.
Unfortunately, this faded after a while, and the
phantom "I" has returned.**

Pure awareness lasted only a few days? This is impossible.
Timeless awareness always is. It doesn't come and go. It is
what you are, always. Did you actually disappear at any
time? Who knew that the experience "came and went",
that it lasted only a few days and then was gone?

That which registered these thoughts is the awareness
that I am talking about, the real you. Whatever came and
went was not awareness.

If you identify with those thoughts, there is seemingly
an appearance of movement, a coming and going with the
thoughts. But has awareness really moved? What is here
witnessing the comings and goings? Innate awareness is
here before, during and after all conceptualizing.

Keep going with the looking and this will eventually
resolve. Keep looking, keep inquiring, into the truth
of your being. Keep exposing the non-existence of the
person you take yourself to be. Be aware of it, notice it,
but do not worry about it. Also notice that the awareness
that sees this supposed fading of itself doesn't actually

fade at all. It's simply that thoughts and stories are once again appearing and disappearing on the screen of awareness, appearing and disappearing in you and upon you. These stories do not define you. You are the space giving rise to and holding all stories.

Do not worry about assigning values to your experiences. Don't bother with analysing or evaluating where you are or how far you have gone. These are just the imaginings of a mind-made character in the storyline.

Whatever view you might have of yourself is a mind-made construct, made up of assumptions and concepts about what you are and what the world is. It's just a dream, a movie comprised of infinite assumptions and concepts. But you are not a concept.

You are that to which and in which all concepts appear. This One that you are looks with loving detachment at all the stories of losing, finding and awakening.

*   *   *

**Why do some enlightened teachers commit
not so enlightened acts?**

Firstly, there are not enlightened people, only enlightened awareness. But for the sake of this discussion, let's pretend that there are enlightened people.

Many have had a deep realization of their true nature, but few have embodied it so much that there are no gaps left between the realization and its outer expression. This is what is sometimes called embodiment or liberation, where actions start to flow from that which was realized.

While embodiment is not necessarily about becoming a moral person, in the words of the Tibetan teacher, Tulku Urgyen Rinpoche, "Your view should be as wide as the sky but your conduct as fine as barley flour."

If we use the energy of our realization and the loftiness of our view as an excuse to fuel and indulge our conditionings, then the ego has co-opted awakening and has turned it into creating its own kingdom where it can once again rule unchallenged.

Recently I received an email asking "If the absolute is the only reality, then who is there to benefit from my good actions?"

This is the great mystery, but only to those of us who still see some difference between the seer and the seen, the enlightened and the unenlightened, the sacred and the profane.

Paradoxically, that's the way the absolute set up the game, so that It, can discover Itself over and over again in and through the manifested world and in and through these impermanent forms of you and me, in which we find ourselves appearing. In truth, we are the absolute, expressing itself as the relative.

Why would the absolute want to express itself in this dreamy impermanent world?

Nisargadatta Maharaj summed it up perfectly when he said, "When I see I am nothing, that is wisdom. When I see I am everything that is love. Between these two my life flows."

And with the realization that the function of the One in the many is love, we realize that we are also love and that love must love and serve all beings, even though ultimately there is no one existing independently from that One, including ourselves.

8
THE SWAY OF EMOTION

"EMOTIONS CANNOT BE PERMANENT.
THAT'S WHY THEY ARE CALLED EMOTIONS.
THE WORD COMES FROM MOTION, MOVEMENT.
THEY MOVE."
– OSHO

One night after gathering firewood, Milarepa, most beloved saint of Tibet, came home to his cave high up in the Himalayas to find it filled with demons.

They had been cooking and eating his food, reading his holy texts, even sleeping in his bed. He immediately saw that they were nothing more than his own mind projections, yet he still wanted to be rid of them, so he tried to subdue them.

They simply laughed at his futile attempt. He continued to try everything in his power to get rid of them, but none of his efforts worked. He then decided to send the demons compassion and love, and though many did leave after this, a handful of the most tenacious ones remained.

When he finally came to see that he really didn't know what to do to clear these last few demons, he let go and sat himself down on the floor, spontaneously inviting them to stay with him as long as they wanted to.

At this moment, every demon except the meanest and most ferocious one left.

Milarepa then deepened and surrendered himself even further, and placing his head into the last demon's mouth said, "So, eat me if you want to."

The demon vanished never to be seen again.

EMOTIONS ARE ENERGIZED THOUGHTS

It is very easy to forget our awakened nature when we are caught in strong emotions, which are energized thoughts, and to either lose perspective or try to escape our distress through distraction or denial.

We may have an idea that "if only we were spiritual enough" we wouldn't be experiencing any suffering from our thoughts and emotions. Our unrealistic expectations make us feel and think that our life is full of distress.

Really seeing the reality of what is here gives us back our sense of perspective and gives us insight into these strong thoughts, into these deep-seated beliefs that are creating our experience.

In order to release these beliefs, we first need to clearly see what is going on right now by paying close attention to what is actually here, including our "I don't want to feel this" or "I should not be feeling this".

The second step is to give the emotions a bit of space, a bit of loving kindness, as you would give to a friend in distress. All they need to dissolve is a little bit of space, because they are usually a bit overcrowded.

Don't indulge them, but give them space and a little bit of compassion, a little bit of time for them to move through you.

LOSE THE CLOUDS AND GAIN THE SKY

In the face of strong emotions, it is easier to see what we are angry about than the actual source of the anger. We flow into the contents of awareness instead of seeing the source of those appearances, which is awareness itself.

If we look beneath the emotions, toward the source of those emotions, we discover an aware and alert spaciousness that doesn't change, that's always there for us, regardless of what happens on the surface.

Try to relax as your thoughts and emotions come and go. Without judging them, try to let go of everything including any thoughts about your emotions.

The more relaxed you become, the more you see the spacious presence/awareness that you are, giving rise to and containing everything, including the emotions you consider "bad" and all the emotions you aspire to have that you consider "good". None of them are you.

When we stay with the actual experience and sensation of any emotion, without trying to change it, escape it or numb to it, we discover that our distress is not solid; it is constantly changing. At the bottom of that strong emotion is just a mix of old beliefs, thoughts and bodily sensations.

Once we see this, our distress begins to unravel by itself, becoming lighter and more transparent. Then the focus of our awareness will naturally expand to include the outer environment.

We will once again start noticing the sunlight streaming through the windows, the song of the birds in the trees, and the remains of our distress will dissolve on its own without us trying to get rid of it.

*   *   *

When a strong emotion like anger or fear takes me over, I lose awareness.

Even during moments of deepest identification with emotions and form, awareness is always present. You have developed the tendency to focus on the contents of awareness rather than the awareness itself. But even though your attention is on the contents of awareness, and you are overlooking the awareness itself, a little clear seeing reveals that awareness has not changed one bit or gone anywhere. How could it? Awareness is what is doing the seeing.

What is aware of the emotions? Look beneath the emotions toward their source and you will discover an aware, alert spaciousness that doesn't change, that's always there for you, regardless of what happens on the surface.

Once you start to see and realize this, the interest and focus on emotions spontaneously subsides. Once you realize that you are the space containing all things, including emotions, you just let them be, you give them space. They are merely fleeting shadows that never actually touch the real you.

*   *   *

I understand that there is nobody here, that there is no separate "I", but I do not feel a sense of joy or peace. Where is the joy I keep reading about?

Be mindful of your contradiction in terms. You cannot say there is no "I" in one sentence and then say, "I do not feel it" or "I am miserable" in the next. How can an "I" that does not exist feel joy or misery? Can you see the contradiction in your concepts here?

True liberation is not about adhering to a new belief that "There is no I", "everything is perfect as it is", "there is nothing to do …" and so on. How can joy or peace arise under the burden of all these concepts? These are just more beliefs to supplant an old belief system. Any set of words by which we measure our success, or lack thereof, is just another set of words that reinforces the mind's limitations.

If something gives you a glimpse of enlightenment or clarity, and your mind tries to claim it as a goal that you have reached, you have still missed the point. This is actually another thought for a non-existent "I" that thinks it has now arrived at its goal. But you cannot reach a point at which you already stand.

The recognition "nobody here/nobody there" is not a cold, empty, heartless space. When you truly realize that there is nobody here and nobody there, you also see that everything appears in this space that you are as the expression of you. Then how can you shut joy out?

You are imagining an enlightened, aware "I" that sees that the "I" is not there, but they are both the same "I". That same "I" has come back in new clothes and proudly announced its absence. You see what's going on here?

This is the story of the infamous enlightened ego. The moment you give interest to the story, however enlightened the story seems to be, you overlook the awareness that is always here. This is the moment where you once again begin to imagine yourself as a separate entity! This being the case, the suffering and doubts will return because you have not truly seen the root of it.

You still believe in an "I" that can be enlightened, but no "I", no matter how enlightened, is you. You are the awareness in which every "I" appears and disappears.

True freedom is when all the stories, all the insights, all the realizations, concepts, beliefs and positions dissolve. What remains is what you are; a vast, conscious, luminous space simply resting in itself. This existence, presence, awareness is what this is all about.

Without truly deeply seeing this, you are missing everything.

*   *   *

**Do you ever get in a bad mood and what do
you do to resolve it?'**

Yes, there are times when I get into a bad mood, but
I don't do anything with it. I know that I am not the bad
feeling or mood, just as I know I am not the thoughts and
sensations that cross the field of the pure awareness that
I am. I don't try to get rid of the mood. I simply allow it to
be, knowing that it will leave of its own accord.

If you feel angry or sad, so what? It doesn't matter
much. Let the feelings come and let them go. This way the
passing emotion doesn't become entrenched in the mental
field, the energy that comes from our mind, our attention.
The more attention, the more it inflates like a balloon.
Moods are not a problem unless they are in relation to
any one entity that is personalizing their experience.

The sky does not care if there are clouds. The clouds
may be light and small, or they may be dark and heavy
with rain, but it does not affect the sky.

Everything constantly changes and there is no problem
with that unless there is a separate entity taking it personally.
Moods will continue as long as the mind and body are
present and functioning, and they are not a problem unless
they get attached to an entity that "has" them.

9

BECOME THE SKY

"OUR INHERENTLY PRESENT WAKEFULNESS IS
NOT SOMETHING WE'LL FIND IN THE FUTURE, NOR
SOMETHING WE HAD IN THE PAST. IT'S PRESENT 'RIGHT
NOW'. AND IT'S SOMETHING THAT WE DON'T HAVE TO
ACCEPT OR REJECT. DON'T DO ANYTHING ABOUT IT: DON'T
ADOPT IT, DON'T AVOID IT, DON'T ENTERTAIN ANY HOPE
OR FEAR ABOUT IT, DON'T TRY TO CHANGE IT OR ALTER IT
OR IMPROVE IT IN ANY WAY."
— TULKU URGYEN RINPOCHE

While I was growing up in Sicily, we had some troublesome relatives that would drop in unexpectedly. My uncle wanted to pretend that no one was home, but my aunty would let them in.

She would be nice, but she wouldn't entertain them too much. Eventually they stopped coming because they were not getting the attention they wanted.

It's the same with thoughts and emotions. Don't chase them or engage with them, and eventually the lack of attention will make them wither away. Then only pure, naked awareness remains, knowing everything as itself.

You will still have emotions arising, thoughts arising, appearances arising, but now you know all manifestation is just awareness appearing as other. They are just impersonal movies that unfold on the screen of awareness. You can now observe the world with detachment, letting the clouds appear and disappear on and in you.

AWARENESS DOESN'T COME AND GO

If your experience is that awareness comes and goes, consider what exactly you are taking to be awareness. If it comes and goes, it cannot be your eternal unchanging natural state. It has to be one of the appearances in awareness.

The idea that your original nature can come and go is just a thought, a misunderstanding. Thoughts, by their nature, come and go endlessly in you. But you are not the thought; you are the one seeing the thought, so any thought of who you are cannot be the truth of who you are.

The habit of always flowing out into thoughts, emotions and outer manifestation distracts us from our natural self and the distractions seemingly cover this awareness. But all that is happening is that attention has flown outward, chasing objects. In reality awareness has not gone anywhere. It is still the background, the perceiving of everything. Without awareness, we wouldn't be aware of anything, including the distractions.

All that needs to be done at this point is to recognize the perceiver, the essence of the thinker. The moment we recognize the essence of the thinker, all thoughts dissolve into the awareness from where they originated.

RECOGNIZE THE ESSENCE OF THE PERCEIVER

Any distraction from simply abiding in present awareness usually starts with the freezing of attention toward something. This something could be an object, a thought or an emotion. It happens because we forget the no-thing aspect of our nature and that there is no separate entity that could grasp anything. But if at this point you become aware that this has happened or is about to happen, in just recognizing this, you are already out of the distraction and awareness is re-established.

When you notice that you are paying attention to

something, you know that you are back in thought. But in realizing this, awareness is present again, conscious of itself again, and the observer is gone.

Just remember that the moment you remember to come back, you are already back. Then you just stop there. Don't try to modify it, prolong it or do anything about it. Just stop. Don't think that you have to "nail awareness down", because that would be a fabricated state, not your natural state.

If our original nature was something tangible, we could train ourselves to hold it by applying mindfulness. But our nature is an intangible no-thing, so the best thing is not to create anything artificial, because the minute we create something that is not spontaneously present, we move away from our original nature.

LIKE A MIRROR ALLOW EVERYTHING TO BE REFLECTED

Simply allow awareness to be naturally stable by not entertaining thoughts. You don't need to do anything but refrain from accepting the invitation to be distracted. This is not about being mindful, where a subject tries not to be distracted by an object, but about leaving the senses wide open, not letting the attention be absorbed by the five senses.

It is like being a mirror, allowing whatever is presented to the senses to be registered without blocking anything and without chasing anything, just as a mirror allows everything to be reflected.

Eventually the distractions will be fewer and fewer, and these uninvited guests will disappear.

When your wakefulness is undistracted and uninterrupted throughout the night and day, this is liberation.

*   *   *

Does your own awareness ever ebb or have variations in depth or strength?

No. Awareness always is, and it can be neither more nor less. Awareness is something that is absolute, without degrees. It is not a relative concept.

My experience is that sometimes it seems as if I am in a deeper state of awareness than at other times – for example, when I am by myself there is just this absolute vastness, absolutely no separation because I don't have to exteriorize myself in order to relate to another. But this is only from the relative viewpoint of the body–mind.

* * *

**I have been a seeker for many years and during the
practice of Instant Presence you recommended, I have
been experiencing the truth of my original nature as an
infinite spaciousness. But, the sense of a subtle
"I" is still there ...**

So now just let that spaciousness go. Why? Because it is
still a mind state.

Our original nature is open, spacious, lucid awareness,
but not as an egoic experience – "Ahh, I am so open,
so vast, so spacious that I encompass the universe of
universes!" We may feel amazingly open and spacious, but
the "I" is still there. This is still a dualistic mind state and
not our real state at all.

Who you truly are is not an object that can be held in
the mind. As soon as the notion of spaciousness arises, the
ego has turned it into an object.

As we deepen into our original nature, it is common to
experience a sense of unconfined spaciousness and this is
a wonderful state. Yes, there can be a huge sense of freedom
in that, but "you" are still there holding and perceiving the
spaciousness. So then you let the spaciousness go.

At some point you may begin to notice that you are
"staying within the spaciousness". So then you let the

"staying" go too. And then you may notice that there is still a very slight desire of wanting the spaciousness again. So you let that go as well, and as you let more and more go of any state where a witness is present, no matter how subtle, all that remains is the spaciousness itself, awareness itself.

PRESENCE PAUSE

AWARENESS IS ALWAYS HERE

While maintaining a relaxed but alert watchfulness, let the thought "awareness comes and goes" arise and watch it carefully without losing yourself in it.

- Is the thought inside the aware intelligence that is the knower of the thought, or is the thought outside of that?

- Is there any difference between the thought itself and the aware intelligence that knows it?

- Stay with the thought and especially watch when the thought ends. Does the awareness witnessing both the movement of the thought and the stillness of no thought change in any way?

Allow, be curious, be open and notice the space in which all thoughts, emotions and manifestations rise and fall. Rest in this simple wakefulness again and again until you are satisfied that awareness is always here in spite of what appears and disappears in and on it.

PART 4

LIVING THE TRUTH OF WHO WE ARE

"WHAT ARE YOU TALKING ABOUT? HAVING TO EARN A
LIVING DOESN'T STOP YOU DIGGING FOR THE TREASURE.
DON'T ABANDON EVERYDAY LIFE. THAT'S WHERE THE
TREASURE IS."
– RUMI

What does the search for enlightenment mean in terms of day-to-day life on planet Earth? How do we live this life, knowing the truth of our essential nature as awareness? Many seekers get so attached to the spiritual path and to the perfection of transcendence that they take refuge in it, away from the world. They become indifferent and may stop caring for anything including themselves. Such individuals may believe that they have reached the top of the mountain but in reality they are just stuck in another mind state. To be fixated on transcendence is just the opposite of being stuck in duality.

With true enlightenment, we no longer see a division between duality and transcendence. The natural consequence of awakened beingness is a clear and simple expression of awareness that never fixates in any realm of experience.

An impersonal love also comes to the fore, an awakened compassion that does not stem from the body–mind unit. Rather, it is the spontaneous expression of the true self, coming from the same source that creates everything moment by moment.

This love or compassion when married with the power of transcendence or wisdom becomes the divine impulse in action for the benefit of all beings. This impulse is the wish and the will to help all sentient beings to the realization of their highest potential, enlightenment.

We are no longer focusing on escaping the world, but neither do we get caught in the trap of trying to fix everything and everyone. When the ego is involved that compassion is usually transmuted into a need that crosses appropriate boundaries whenever seeking to help others. It can give rise to an attitude of superiority that sees others as pitiful and lost, and can become tyrannical and controlling to those it is trying to help.

But when we no longer see a division between "us" and "them", we offer our help where it seems appropriate and allow it to take root where it needs to grow.

This natural intelligence, love and compassion is not an act that we do; it is what we are. We understand the play of appearances – and yet ... we take action.

10

TO DIE BEFORE WE DIE

"DIE WHILE YOU ARE ALIVE, AND BE ABSOLUTELY DEAD.
THEN DO WHATEVER YOU WANT: IT'S ALL GOOD."
— SHIDŌ BUNAN

Right now as I write, my cat, Shimla, is sleeping peacefully on the chair near the heater. My other cat, Pushkar, strolls in and, with a graceful roll of his body, lies face up on the warm pavement in front of the heater with a blissed-out look on his face, totally unconcerned about what may happen next. If death should come the next moment, so be it. There is no concern. He is too busy living life moment by moment to be concerned with the future, totally releasing one moment and welcoming the next.

As human beings, we are very rarely in the present moment. Rather we tend to be "lost in our thoughts", one moment thinking about our past and the next about our future.

If we stop chasing past and future, we land in the present moment, here and now. From here, death is happening in every moment. One moment subsides and that is the death of that moment. Then another moment arises and that is the birth of another moment.

The truth is that we go through birth and death continually. They take place every moment.

Learning to recognize this moment-to-moment birth and death is to go behind our ideas and concepts about death.

The essence of death is discovered in the gap between one moment ceasing and another one beginning. That essence is the wakefulness that is our true nature.

FACING THE FEAR OF DEATH

Death and dying are taboo topics in the western world. While we all know the inevitability of death and the fear that it inspires, this is not a reality we like to face. We would rather deny, repress and run from death. This, however, will not help much because, in the end, death always catches up with us.

Death was part of the contract when we accepted the idea of birth, and facing death before we die gives us the choice to rediscover the awareness and the love that will guide us when we have to confront this most feared moment of our lives.

Our bodies progress from childhood to adulthood to old age. But there is something within us that never changes, never becomes anything other than what it has always been. This is the truth of the essential self. It is who we are when we are born, what remains unchanging as our bodies age, and it will still be the same when we die. The only thing that changes is the appearance and there is no appearance that can touch what we really are.

ONLY THE FORM CHANGES

Our bodies are temporary vehicles and they appear and disappear in the awareness that we always are. No matter how many billions and billions of bodies come and go, awareness remains unchanged. The appearance may shift, but our awareness and being are still the same.

Only the form changes, like you would change your shirt. Consider an outfit you used to like. You wore it, looked good in it, were comfortable in it, and when it no longer served its purpose or become worn out, you threw it away. Our bodies are like that, but our true nature, as awareness, is not altered by death. If we let our minds wander to envision ourselves beyond death, we lose sight of our true nature as ever-present awareness. Time is a concept in awareness, and it is created by the mind. But awareness exists outside of time, independent of bodies coming and going, unconcerned with any temporary appearance.

WHAT DOES DEATH MEAN TO YOU, DEEP DOWN, IN YOUR GUT, NAKEDLY?

How we define death is how we will experience death and this is an important question that will guide us in how to die well. To die well, we need to learn to live well.

Living well is learning to die every day, every moment, to our thoughts, to our emotions, even to our life. Only by learning to die to everything can we meet life and death fully.

Every story comes to an end. Every moment comes to an end. What we call our life and our story is just one moment after another, a million moments succeeding one another, giving the illusion of continuity.

If we look closer, we see that this continuity is illusory and that each single moment is born and then dies, and then is born again like the ocean's waves. The "I" in the story with which we identify also arises and dissolves each moment. Watch closely and notice that the "I" of this moment disappears when the next moment arrives and the next "I" is born ever fresh, ever new. Only the mind strings them together as the same continuous self.

By observing this continuous ebb and flow, we start to understand how death and life are intimately connected. We see that it is only through death that something new can be born. Life without death would be a state frozen in eternity. No reality, no creativity, no new discovery would be possible.

By learning how to die in each moment, we discover that with each death there is rebirth and that only by releasing our grasp on the continuity of our own individual existence do we have the opportunity to see the luminous space from which all forms are born and die. Then our mind relaxes, becoming open and accepting of the inevitable changes and deaths that are part of any life. Welcoming the sensation of fear with complete openness slowly softens the barriers that we have created with our habitual patterns.

WE ARE THE ONE THAT WITNESSES DEATH

Investigate the natural life cycle of one single moment. It doesn't have to be any moment in particular; you can use your next moment.

Watch the moment being born, watch it live and watch it die. Take note of what happens when that moment dies. Do you die? Notice how awareness is totally and completely present when each moment dies. This Eternal Presence is the only constancy, all else is temporal.

In recognizing the illusion of continuity, we have the opportunity to stop fearing death and to know the deeper reality that exists underneath and beyond death. We realize that we are not the one that is frightened. We are That which is witnessing fear. We are not the one who dies; we are the one that witnesses death.

Then we are no longer afraid of death because we know that death is not apart from the life that we are, and that only That which is able to renew itself is truly eternal.

*   *   *

I want to face my fear of death now, before the body dies, but how do I do that?

We think that the fear of death is the fear of the unknown, but this is not true. Our fear of death is our grasping of what we know.

As long as your identity is being defined as a body, you will be fearful of losing that body. So the solution is: turn your attention away from the dream character you are identifying with right now. Observe the character as if it were part of a dream and watch how the character interacts within this dream. Now, shift your focus and attention to the awareness that is observing the character. This is the awareness that is always present and does not change no matter what happens to the character.

If any form moves, changes, makes an appearance and then disappears, then you can be sure that it is not awareness. It is merely one of an infinite array of forms that awareness assumes.

So even all of the shifts and deep transformations that occur in the life of the made-up character are simply the arbitrary ways in which energy moves across the motionless face of awareness. Movements of energy in the story of a non-existent character, like waves arising and falling in the awareness that we are.

Awareness is the one essence that assumes an infinite variety of forms. All notions of past and future, here and there, you and I, and this or that are simply ideas that arise out of the vast ocean of awareness.

You are the deep, vast ocean of awareness and experiences, including the experience of death, are the waves that are constantly moving across its (your) surface.

You are this awareness, which has no mortality, no vulnerability and no limits.

*   *   *

What are your thoughts concerning reincarnation?

As long as we believe ourselves to be separate individuals, there are endless concepts, beliefs, ideas and doctrines about life. Ideas like reincarnation are engaging to those who see themselves as separate seekers, because they provide a plausible explanation for their existence. But the real point is: are we really born? Do we know conclusively that who we are ever really dies? And what, if anything, is left over to reincarnate?

There is no need to investigate, prove or disprove all the various mechanics and theories concerning reincarnation, but it is important to remember that through it all, only awareness exists and everything is this. Perhaps physical matter can be recycled and maybe thought energy can be used again, but you remain what you already are.

You are like a bottomless sea, infinite and eternal and your presence is timeless. If the ocean gives rise to waves that then change into other waves, that is fine, but the waves do not exist separately from the sea. It is all water and it all returns to water. The water itself does not change.

Instead of wasting time wondering what one was in a previous life or what one will be in the next life, why don't you investigate what you are right now?

* * *

**If awareness exists beyond this body, why can't
I remember anything that happened before I was
born into this body?**

Your body–mind is the instrument of awareness and that which allows perception, but it cannot have memories of things that happened before it appeared. Let's say, for example, that you have recently acquired a new camera. Would the film in that camera contain images from before the camera was created?

Each body–mind instrument will have a different perspective of events, just as you would have if you were to place two different cameras in two slightly different places to record the same event.

Your body–mind is just a single object among endless objects that appears in awareness. Awareness is the source of these appearances and what makes possible the perception of the body and world around you.

11

LIVE WHERE YOU FEAR TO LIVE

"AS A BEE SEEKS NECTAR FROM ALL KINDS OF FLOWERS,
SEEK TEACHINGS EVERYWHERE.
LIKE A DEER THAT FINDS A QUIET PLACE TO GRAZE,
SEEK SECLUSION TO DIGEST ALL THAT YOU HAVE GATHERED.
LIKE A MAD ONE BEYOND ALL LIMITS, GO WHERE YOU PLEASE
AND LIVE LIKE A LION COMPLETELY FREE OF ALL FEAR."
– DZOGCHEN TANTRA

There once lived a king who was presented with a special gift of two peregrine falcons from Arabia. They were the most magnificent creatures the King had ever seen. Passing the precious birds over to his head falconer, he requested that the two birds be fully trained.

After several months, the head falconer returned and let it be known to the king that although one of the birds was now soaring gloriously through the air, he had not managed to succeed with the other bird which hadn't moved off its branch since the day it had arrived. On hearing this, the king immediately summoned all the sorcerers and healers in the land to tend to the bird to make it fly, but even they failed to move it from its perch. After considering the situation more closely, the king realized that what he needed to do was find someone who was more familiar with the way of birds in their natural environment to truly understand the problem. "Go and fetch me a farmer," he commanded his court.

The next morning the king was thrilled to see the falcon gliding through the sky high above the palace gardens. "Bring me this miracle maker!" he exclaimed to his court.

The court immediately found the farmer and brought him before the king.

"How did you manage to make the falcon fly?" the king asked.

Humbly bowing his head, the farmer replied, "It was very easy your Highness, I simply cut off the branch that the bird was sitting on."

WE WERE BORN TO FLY

We are all born to fly. Instead, we sit on the branches afraid of the leap into the unknown. But the unknown is where enlightenment lives. Our true nature is the unknown.

As children, we were all small, fearless ones, and nothing was too great for us. But then the world started telling us, "Who do you think you are? You can't do that. You can't be that." We bought into it and then we also started telling ourselves the same lie.

To reclaim our greatness, we need to go against the collective unconscious that has taught us to fit in, to not break the mould or rock the boat, to play small.

We think we are afraid of death, but an even greater fear is that of truly living. Fear of failing, fear of achieving our potential and fear of what others will think of us are probably the three biggest fears that contribute to the "fear of our greatness".

Only by reconnecting with that which animates the body–mind can we start to truly glimpse our own innate greatness, which is similar to standing in the sun. The light warms and illuminates us, but it also has the potential to burn us. However, as Victor Frankl stated, "Those who would shine must learn to endure burning."

It is our natural birthright to be great. There is nothing we need to do, get or know to be what we are.

If we can sit with this and let everything unfold from this knowing, it will destroy the branches of fear and attachment that we cling to. It will free us to experience the glory of flight into the realm of infinite eternal awareness.

DEVELOPING TRUST

I remember learning to swim as a child; it took courage to let go and trust that if I relaxed, the water would support me and I wouldn't drown. I surrendered enough to allow myself to float in the shallow water.

One day, soon after I learned to float, I was on a boat with my dad. Without warning, he threw me into the deep water. His own father had done this to him when he was a child to teach him to swim.

At first I was shocked and I panicked as I started ingesting water but before my dad could pull me out, I relaxed and surrendered to the water and easily floated to the surface, never fearing water again.

TURN TOWARD THE FEAR

Living where you fear to live doesn't take courage, it takes trust. Some people, like my mother, never learned to swim because they never learned to trust. Yet we can only trust when we have tasted our own true nature, knowing that in truth, we cannot die. The only thing that will die is what we are not, all the ideas about who we are. These are the very ideas to which we tightly hang onto because the entity we believe to be, the ego, gets scared and asks "Who will I be then?"

The ego is a very fragile thing because it is a false thing, and as such it needs to have something to hold on to (thoughts, beliefs, fears) or it may die. This is why it is so afraid; death could come to it at any moment.

Ultimately it is the Truth of your being that uses fear to push Itself to Its own awakening, so don't turn away from it. Turn toward it, face it and see if it can hurt you. You will find that it can't. From then on, life becomes simple, easy and spontaneous as you realize that it is not you as the ego who moves through life, but that life flows before you, and you are the immutable awareness containing it all.

*   *   *

I truly, desperately want enlightenment but I am also completely terrified by it.

It's the ego that has put this fear into your mind. Enlightenment is awakening from the ego, so of course there will be fear involved in this. Obviously, the ego is afraid of its own death.

The irony is that the ego can search for enlightenment, God and the absolute reality, but when it comes close to it, it turns back, terrified because it starts to realize that at the (imaginary) finish line of enlightenment, there is no reward or prize for itself but death.

Fear is actually a very good sign that we are getting close to the truth of our being. Before coming face to face with the real self, we always meet our deepest fear – the fear of losing ourselves, of disappearing, of death.

The next time fear shows its face, look at the root of the fearful entity with curiosity and courage. Look at the fear, and the one who is fearful and the awareness that is observing the whole thing. Where are you in all this?

*   *   *

Nisargadatta talked mainly about the "I am" but he told us that there is more … This last step is still incomprehensible to me …

The realization of the "I am" is an advanced realization and many will stop here to enjoy living as the universal beingness. Only very few rare ones keep going past this lofty state and come to realize that even beingness is still a form of duality.

This step is sometimes called the great death or even the great suicide because to move past this stage, we need to give up the high identity as the universal "I am" and surrender the final and terrifying realization that "there is nothing".

This "nothing" is not an absence, but a "something" which is not a thing; pure awareness unaware of Itself. This is the ultimate reality, the final step.

*   *   *

The "great suicide" doesn't sound very inspiring ...

It's relatively easy to give up our limited identity of the body–mind for the identity of "Universal Consciousness". But how many can give that up, how many can give up the very sense of beingness itself?

Nisargadatta said, "We *love* to be." Above all, we "want to be".

So of course contemplating "not being anymore", when looked at from the position of the mind, seems like absolute annihilation and who in their right mind wants to be completely annihilated?

Only the true sage will take this evolutionary final step and allow this annihilation so that only That which was always there shines through.

12

WE TASTE ONLY SACREDNESS

"MANY FEEL THAT A PERSON WHO SPENDS HIS TIME
SOUL-SEARCHING IS MORE HOLY THAN A MERCHANT
WHO HAWKS HIS GOODS AT THE MARKET. A HIGHLY
SPIRITUAL PERSON IS ACTUALLY ONE WHO HAS FOUND
THE COMFORT ZONE THAT EXISTS SOMEWHERE
BETWEEN THE TWO EXTREMES."
– HAROLD KLEMP

When I was a child, I'd look at myself in the mirror and I'd feel so out of place. I would frequently wonder, what am I doing here in this strange body with arms and legs and this funny face? Now, I am happy being in this body. What an amazing thing it is to be in this body; eating delicious food, going out into the garden, seeing flowers, meeting myself again and again everywhere I look.

Even though now it is realized to be a dream, it feels like the most amazing, precious gift that out of all the infinite possibilities I am here now, in this body, in this life. The impermanence of life makes it all the more precious. This simple ordinary feeling of being here now is the biggest miracle of all.

IN TRUE AWAKENING, NOTHING STANDS APART AND NOTHING IS EXCLUDED

There is a popular Zen tale known by many. A rough translation would be something like this: "Before I started Zen, there were valleys and mountains. Once I started Zen, the valleys and mountains vanished. When I was truly awake, the mountains and valleys returned."

If we were to break down the above journey into different "stages", the first stage is referring to a normal state of consciousness in which the world "out there" is full of separate things. We are one of those separate things "in here" on our way to awakening "out there".

The second stage where the valleys and mountains vanish is realizing that there is no "in here" and there is no "out there".

Each of us, and everything around us, is one. We may be different, but we are one, just like the facets of an uncut gem. From this viewpoint, it can be seen that Hitler and Ramana Maharshi are aspects of One Being. Though there are many experiences in life, they are all of the same fabric. At this stage we are tasting the Absolute, the realization that all is One.

With the third stage, true awakening, the valleys and mountains return, yet we no longer need to hold on tight to the Absolute nor to avoid or deny our ordinary human existence. While we see that Hitler and Ramana Maharshi are aspects of one reality, we still see that there is also a gigantic difference between them.

The truth that there is only the "One" is understood, yet there is also involvement in time, a history and a goal-setting for the future.

We are infinite awareness and we are also the mind-made entity. Just like the two sides of a coin, both sides are different and both sides are true.

REALIZATION INCLUDES EVERYTHING

Awakening, or enlightenment, is both everything and nothing. It is all beings and the individual. It is being open and being closed. It is accepting all manifestation as an expression of oneself.

Waking up to transcendental reality, emptiness, the space where everything abides, is only half of the truth. We can become so absorbed in this perspective that we can't function in the world, we can't keep a job or look after our family or ourselves.

Realization includes everything, the mundane and the transcendental. In true awakening, nothing stands apart and nothing is excluded. If we find ourselves in a state where something is excluded, that state, however amazing it is, is still a dualistic state.

TASTING THE SACRED

Once a spiritual teacher asked me, "Could this moment be any more perfect than it is?"

When we are ripe, we immediately know the simple answer to this question. How could this moment be any more or any less than it is? Yet, so much of our effort focuses on moving somewhere else, being somewhere else, attaining more or wanting less of what is. But can this moment be any more perfect than it is?

Any attempt to make it more perfect creates and perpetuates our separateness.

The gap between what is and what we want it to be is the only thing that separates us from the Truth of our being. This gap is only a mind construct. As soon as we recognize the gap, the search is over and this is where we taste the sacred, in this moment just as it is.

DON'T MISS A MOMENT

We usually approach the moment with so many expectations, concepts and judgements that our spontaneous openness to accept each moment as it is, is limited. We are so focused on the transcendental that we forget we are living on Earth. We live in the world but pine for heaven. But the two are not separate. They are One.

LIFE IS THE EXPRESSION OF PURE AWARENESS

If this present moment of wakefulness is left as it is, it is pure awareness. If this moment of wakefulness is altered in any way (eg moves toward a thought, object, etc) then it becomes our ordinary mind, which also perceives, because it is made of the same substance as the wakefulness, yet now it is manifesting subject/object duality.

Awareness at rest is emptiness. This is the truth of who we are.

Awareness in movement is all form, all life, all manifestation. This also is the truth of who we are.

When we realize this, our very existence starts to have a deep value and meaningfulness.

Our lives are a divine expression no matter how messy and weird they may be. How much more meaningful can it get? The source is experiencing itself in form in a conscious, awake way.

We realize that our purpose has been to wake up from form so that we can finally come consciously into form.

We realize that the essence of life is manifesting through the body–mind, which has become a channel, a vehicle through which awareness can flow with less distortion.

Osho said, "Enlightenment is the understanding that this is all, that this is perfect, that this is it."

In this very moment, now, the one reading these words, your life, now, the light and the dark, whatever is occurring, whatever it may be, that in itself is the key. Recognizing the miraculous immediacy and beauty in the very moment of every experience, just as it is, is it.

*   *   *

Four months ago I had an encounter with emptiness but instead of being a joyous experience it has left me with feeling of "what's the point ... it's all empty anyway."

Real emptiness or awareness is what you are, not an object of perception, and I believe this might be how you're categorizing it. You are looking at emptiness from the perspective of the mind.

When the mind looks at emptiness, all it sees is darkness, an abyss and meaninglessness. The fear and anxiety you are feeling is the mind trying to locate itself in this abyss.

Your sense of meaninglessness – "it is all empty anyway" – is the disillusionment the ego feels because it once had high hopes and expectations that awakening was going to bring a life of bliss and delight for itself. But awakening is the last and biggest disappointment for the ego, the end of all its dreams and grand expectations.

As the illusion of the ego entity starts to disappear, you feel empty because you have been filled by it for so long, but slowly, even the absence of the ego will disappear and then you will be truly empty with an emptiness that is really full.

Allow the mind to relax and dissolve in the emptiness, then you will find yourself looking out from the emptiness, as the emptiness itself.

*   *   *

**When a concerted effort is made to question reality
the mind can throw up many mysterious "visions"
relating to the senses which in Buddhism includes
consciousness. So when one experiences
Emptiness how is it verified as true? Secondly what
is in that Emptiness?**

Nothing is in the Emptiness. Emptiness is *empty*.

Emptiness is not a thing, an absolute or a special realm of existence. It is not an object of perception but a mode of perception where we look at everything with no thought of whether there's anything lying behind them, empty of the ideas and the stories we usually add to our experience in order to make sense of it.

The experience of Emptiness is verified as true by the unique "aroma" of nothingness: nothing appears other than emptiness.

When we first realize emptiness, we can do so conceptually through an image. By continuing to experience emptiness over and over again, the image gradually becomes more and more transparent until it disappears completely and we see emptiness directly. One never stands apart from emptiness beholding it from somewhere else.

The taste of emptiness in the body, mind and spirit, is the knowingness that what happens is just what happens. You see directly that everything is empty, like misty smoke or like the blue sky, floating and forming and reforming in a vast endless sky. We feel the cloud-like nature of thoughts, emotions, desires, body, actions and words. If we look at anything it disappears like a cloud, and the cloud disappears into a cloud.

We realize that all is emptiness but this doesn't mean we are apart from life. Quite the opposite in fact: it is impossible not to be connected with everything and nothing is beyond our concern. The only thing real is connection: emptiness touching emptiness, free and yet non-different from our self.

When we begin to understand and to live in this way, the sense of alienation from a reality existing as separate from us is gone. The sense of a solid, separate self is gone. The anxiety we may have experienced about the spiritual puzzle "Am I experiencing Emptiness or is this illusion?" is gone. We know that there is no ultimate truth or view to claim, including a view from nowhere. There is no place to land or stand and so there is no place to fall.

*   *   *

From the absolute viewpoint there is nothingness but from the relative, there are things, people and a world we live in. What is the connection between the two?

There is only one viewpoint, the absolute one, because the relative is contained in the absolute. It is only the mind that sees objects, people and a world superimposed on the absolute viewpoint.

The Absolute doesn't see things as separate from Itself, so it can't even be called a "viewpoint". The Absolute looks out and sees that It is everything.

The connection between the two is Love. When we let go, truly let go, it always comes back to this. Love is really another word for awareness.

First we see everything in manifested duality as a "separate other". Then from within the emptiness, we see everything as our "self", just pure oneness with no distinctions whatsoever. Only from this oneness then see that, despite the oneness, there are still "others" appearing separate and independent not as an illusion but as the non-dual reality of "self and other" just as it is.

The playground of the mind is not separate from the Absolute, so the ultimate point of the spiritual path is not to just awaken and live a life of never-ending bliss in the transcendental state, but also to cultivate our own awakened heart and use our life to help everyone we meet, moment-by-moment. It's not just to ask "Who am I?" but to also ask "How can I help?"

Helping can take the form of simply giving our full attention to the people around us or donating money to a worthy cause or working for peace. We can start by identifying our gifts so that we contribute to the world in our own unique way.

We don't have to start big and we don't have to travel anywhere. Right now in our own life there are at least a dozen ways we can help.

We start small, where we are and where they are, right now.

PRESENCE PAUSE

WHY AM I?

Open up to unconditional awareness and then turn your attention to the question: *Why Am I?*

You will notice that your mind will immediately supply an answer or many answers. Resist the temptation to accept or reject and go deeper into the question and if your attention is unmovable and undistracted, you will find that at a certain point the question will disappear and the space that is left is the answer. Not an intellectual answer, but an energy that connect you to That which embodies it.

EPILOGUE

BE AS YOU ARE

"LOVE SAYS, 'I AM EVERYTHING.' WISDOM SAYS, 'I AM
NOTHING.' BETWEEN THE TWO, MY LIFE FLOWS."
– NISARGADATTA MAHARAJ

I look up at the grapevine outside the kitchen door and notice a solitary sparkling drop of rainwater on a vine leaf, shimmering, glistening like crystal, reflecting the early rays of the morning sun. This one drop glistens back to me ... I am that drop.

I see many drops, all reflecting the morning sun, silently whispering their only purpose: to be here and nourish the vine leaf with its moisture, with its juice, and to reflect the source of all life, the Sun Itself. Why? Not because it wants to, or it has to or it desires to, but simply because that's its nature. It simply can't help but reflect the Sun's light; it's in its nature to do so.

What is in our nature that is as simple, clear and uncomplicated as this drop of rain simply reflecting the Sun's rays? The answer cannot be worked out in the mind; it's not something we have to manifest because it's already manifested, wide awake as our true nature.

Simply look up/out/in and see what is shining gloriously, reflecting out, effortlessly, into the world.

This needs no work, requires no preparation, just the willingness to see through all our ideas about what it could be. It sits out in the open waiting to be seen. It's in its nature to be seen as part of the reflecting it does naturally as a constant outpouring. Simply see it and joy will be the outcome.

BEING PRESENT WITH WHAT IS ALREADY PRESENT

Maybe you picked up this book because you thought it could give you something you don't already have, that it could fill a lack, that it might help you get enlightened. By now, however, my hope is that you have realized that there is nothing this book or any book can give you regarding the truth of your being. What you seek you already are. The seeker you believe yourself to be is a concept, an assumption, and it has nothing to do with what you truly are.

To expose the ego's bag of tricks, to finally end the greatest deception of all time, to simply pull the pin on it all and watch the house of cards come tumbling down at your feet requires courage and the willingness to really want to see the truth.

As the cards continue to fall, I invite you to meet head-on the irresistible temptation to start building again, to once again create a "someone" to be. Muster the courage to resist this temptation.

Where does one find this courage? It won't be found in the "me" that is trying to rebuild itself. You must look to the clear, ever-present beingness that simply watches it all. Keep coming back to this.

Allow for the no-gap between "what is" and "what you are" to simply be. Don't try to be it, don't try to get to it; don't try to do anything at all. You already are it; so don't be tempted to make it a thing or to make it yours.

Simply allow for the infinite awareness, the only constant, to reveal itself as forever here. Simply see This, from This, as This.

There is no question of whether or not you already are this awareness. Instead, the question is, do you recognize it?

While we all have unlimited opportunities to recognize this, we consistently miss the moment. If you seem to be missing it right now, simply keep looking and it will open up for you.

Even if you are still holding onto your concepts, still searching, you are and will always be *that*. Who you truly are is simply expressing itself as "the seeker that is searching for something".

All that exists is awareness, and you are that, freedom, liberation itself.

No words can ever come close to your own direct encounter with the magnificence of your own being. Words can only point to it.

If the pointers in this book have, even for an instant, allowed for self-recognition to awaken or, in some small way, a recognition or realization has stirred clarity – then this book has done its job.

Now it is up to you. Let the joy of your own presence lead the way from here to here ... forever here.

In my offering lies your offering. As we each awaken into the awareness that we already are, we meet the world. And in this meeting, truth continues to manifest for the simple joy of itself and the simple love of itself.

Honour this, love this, be this.

This is all.

INTERVIEW WITH ENZA VITA

The following teachings were recorded in Adelaide in September–October 2013 over the course of an introductory six weeks "Practising the Presence" meditation workshop.

*   *   *

When and how did you start on the spiritual path?

ENZA: When I was 17, I left Italy and came to live in Australia on my own. This seemed like an attempt to rebel against authority and to step into the unknown. At the time, I felt that I needed to find something that I didn't yet have.

After a few days in Alice Springs, walking along the main street, I noticed in a shop window one of two symbols that I had been drawing since I was a little girl – a lotus flower on the cover of a large book displayed in the window. Even though I couldn't read English, I went in and bought the book. I went home and painstakingly started deciphering every word with the aid of my Italian–English dictionary I had brought with me from Sicily. This was the start of my outer spiritual journey. Since that day, I have read many spiritual books, joined many spiritual teachings and dabbled in many spiritual practices.

Even though I got "spiritual experiences" from some of these practices, I knew that this was not it. What I was looking for had to be much simpler.

At some point, there was the recognition which is sometimes called "awakening". Space and time stopped and "my life" and "my history" disintegrated.

Identifying myself as someone located in this body–mind stopped. I realized that I had always known this but somehow, as a child, I had accepted the rules of the society I lived in and learned to overlook it and pretend I didn't know it.

Did you have any spiritual experiences or inclinations when you were young?

ENZA: I did but I didn't give them much importance.

Could you give us some examples of the type of experiences you had as a child?

ENZA: Sometimes I would wake up in the morning and be greeted by a vast, alive blissful space. I was filled with this energy flowing in my body like surging waves, an extremely pleasurable ecstasy, a feeling of orgasmic ecstasy that was "everywhere" and "in" everything and "as" everything. I would flow like liquid mercury from one place to another, dizzy with delight and everything I looked at was radiantly beautiful.

Also I seemed to have prophetic dreams, lucid dreams, dream teachings with "maroon-robed monks" and occasionally dreams within dreams where I would lie awake in the morning wondering if I was awake or still in a dream.

I remembered once waking in my parents' bedroom, reaching to touch my mum and suddenly jerking awake in my own bed. *Was I really awake now or was I still dreaming?* I extended my arm, just reaching over to touch my bedside lamp. But the lamp wasn't by my bedside and the sensation of movement woke me up once again. Then I started to free-fall into endless space. *Is this the last level?* I thought for one heart-stopping moment, before I disappeared.

I know that you have studied with teachers of many different spiritual traditions from Dzogchen to Advaita, Zen and Sufism and many others. How have these teachings influenced what you teach today?

ENZA: There is no greater gift a teacher can offer the student than the inspiration to uncover that potential within themselves and my life was changed through that exchange. It gave me the opportunity to see the One Truth that is the essence of all things and it taught me not to cling to one way, one idea, one expression of it.

I have had some past lives where I did lock myself in one viewpoint, fixed ideas about the Truth and I made a vow never to repeat that experience. I vowed to find and share with others the One Truth shining at the core of every path.

To see that One Truth in so many different traditions has been a great gift and a great blessing and I am deeply grateful to all the amazing teachers who have guided and inspired me on my path. My life rests firmly on the foundation of their transmission, but I can't really claim to be transmitting any of these particular traditions.

Nisargadatta told us to find our own path because "Unless you find it yourself, it will not be your own way and will take you nowhere". So, what I am teaching is my own way, the one that worked for me, so in a sense I am biased, but every teacher is, because every teacher teaches what has worked for them.

How would you describe your teaching?

ENZA: My teaching is purely about awakening and my intention is to capture the heart of these traditions, stripped-down of the beautiful but sometimes limiting cultural and religious baggage. Even though at the time I was going through my spiritual training, I could see the reason for them, I didn't feel drawn to that. And I strongly feel that there is a real need for teachers who are not into a traditional religion. A lot of people who contact me are really interested in becoming more aware, but don't want any of the rituals and traditions.

Today, as part of my teaching, I may use some of the methods I have learned from these teachings; there are many methods we can use, but I am not attached to any particular one. You need to tune in to the person in front of you and nudge him or her to discover for themselves what's really important and what is needed for their next step. It's very important for a teacher not to force anything on students but to help the students discover what they need for themselves ...

I've come to realize that being told what we are supposed to do doesn't tell us much about ourselves and that if we're given the chance, the Self we all partake of will come to the fore and exceed all our expectations.

Could you explain the practice you teach? These days there are so many ideas about meditation and spiritual practice that it is very confusing for someone starting on the path.

ENZA: The biggest misunderstanding about meditation and spiritual practice is that you should do something when you meditate. But natural meditation is not about doing anything. Natural meditation is an un-doing. Basically it's a relaxing, a resting, while being alertly aware.

I will give you an example: right in this moment, just notice the awakeness that is looking through your eyes, there is an aware intelligence that allows you to notice everything around this room, including yourself. You can get a sense of this by first simply looking out through your eyes and then "looking back" at that which is doing the looking. Just look right now, don't take my word for it.

This is the practice in a nutshell. To notice what this wakefulness is and to rest in it as long as you can. At first, we may only be able to rest in this aware presence for a few seconds before we are distracted by thoughts. Every time you get distracted, simply bring the attention back toward awareness itself. Relax into this aware presence many times throughout the day. Continue to be aware of that, and soon the distractions will be a thing of the past.

What is your motivation for teaching?

ENZA: I simply speak, knowing full well that this that I talk about can never be touched with words ... and yet there is this impulse coming from this beingness ... This beingness is constantly making love to everything ... the air we breathe, the carpet, the water in that bottle ... everything. And it's incredibly ecstatic, incredibly beautiful and, I guess, it wants to awaken whoever may be interested in awakening.

My motivation is to share this with others, not because I want to but because I have to. I feel the yearning like a lover does, to share this with everyone. To share this so that everyone can feel this.

Some traditions suggest that years of spiritual practice are necessary before one becomes enlightened, but you say that this is not necessary ...

ENZA: This is a misunderstanding of my words. While it's true that we are always the Self, if this hasn't been truly and directly realized, this knowledge won't do us any good.

If this is where we are, it is really important to keep coming back to it until it's effortless to be natural.

How do you know when you have reached the ultimate? How is progress assessed on the spiritual path?

ENZA: At first "progress" is assessed by the degree of our inner expansion, but as we enter more deeply into progressively more subtle and transparent inner territory, it becomes increasingly difficult to assess the nature of our experience because progress here is measured by the dissolution of the self into the Absolute.

What happens to the ego or little self in the moment
of enlightenment?

ENZA: There is not an ego or little self and a higher one. Enlightenment is the direct realization that we are the awakeness that's experiencing every moment of the dream, including the ego character. What you call the little self is not an aware being. The only aware being is the One Being in all beings.

What about thoughts? Where do they arise?

ENZA: All thoughts, including all emotions, arise in that One Being in which everything shares in.

Why would thoughts or emotions like anger or grief
arise in the perfection of that One Beingness? Does
this still happen to you? Do you still get angry or sad?

ENZA: Of course. What we are in essence includes everything – our humanity and being human involves having thoughts and feelings. This is not something to be abolished, but to be fully experienced. Enlightenment does not abolish one's humanity, but actually makes one more human because nothing is resisted.

It's a delusion to think that we can clear up everything so that only beautiful thoughts and emotions remain.

In this world and in this body there are both positive and negative experiences, but they are both coming from here [points inward] which is beyond both.

With enlightenment, the subjective self may still arise but some part of us always knows that this experience is just a wave called "I/me" or Enza or John, not a separate particle called self. The viewpoint that there is a particle inside this body–mind called self disappears at enlightenment.

When we are emptiness, when we realize that everything is emptiness, then we can be everything.

When we meet so-called enlightened people, we always imagine them as having something which the ordinary person in the street doesn't have ...

ENZA: That distinction between an "enlightened person" and the ordinary person is not at all real. I never see some people as "enlightened", myself included, while others are not.

Enlightenment is not something we can achieve because enlightenment is what one already is. Every one of us lives from exactly the same place, living from who we really are – every one of us, but some of us are not using that gift. It's like having a bag of jewels in our pocket and not knowing about it.

The moment that we contemplate the idea that there is someone or something in us that can find this elusive thing called awareness or enlightenment, in that moment we have created a separation, a gap between us and It.

Then we try to remove that gap by having ideas like "I already have it, I am already enlightened because I am already the Self, Awareness, God, the Essence of everything". But there was never a gap in the first place apart from a thought and an idea.

The Self is ever-present – to seek it or long for it is to seemingly deny its presence here and now.

No effort can take us to the true Self. In fact, it takes a lot of effort to pretend not to be this Self. And that is what the imaginary "I" is – the effort of pretending to be something other than this ever-present awareness.

Let our efforts instead bring us repeatedly to this aware space until they arise less and less, leaving us simply here, silent, open and unknowing. That is our true original effortless stateless state.

How does one start?

ENZA: We can awaken only in this moment and everyone can manage an awakened moment. Any moment in which clarity takes the place of confusion, insight displaces delusion and love and compassion dislodges hatred and selfishness is a moment when we are awake. And if we can manage a moment of wakefulness, why not another?

Does enlightenment happen by effort or grace?

ENZA: Enlightenment happens by *itself* when all ideas and concepts of the mind are released (including the energy behind thinking), when all the wants and needs are released (including the want of enlightenment). It "happens" to itself by the blessing of itself on itself. Does that make sense? I hope not ... [laughter]

Is there a final truth, Enza?

ENZA: Look up to the sun; it shines down upon you effortlessly. Look down to the ground; your feet are already on the path. Look into your heart and find that enlightenment is already there. Come back home and realize that you were there all the time!

A SECRET SKY WITHIN

by Enza Vita

This secret seeing is the space,
where the real meets what is not.

It sees all things, knows all things
the seen, the unseen and the not-yet-seen.

Live from this, as this, now,
don't wait for that special moment.

Remove nothing, add nothing, seek nothing,
simply look from this place, through these eyes.

This secret seeing is not yours to get
it is a gift to you from That which sees.

ABOUT THE AUTHOR

ENZA VITA is the publisher and editor of *InnerSelf* newspaper and *Woman Spirit* magazine, and the founder and director of the *MahaShanti Foundation*, a non-profit organization dedicated to the spiritual awakening of all beings.

She has spent over 40 years of her life searching and studying under many of the great spiritual teachers of our age, and has been exposed to the wonderful writings of many others around the world.

As a result she was able to discover the universal teaching underlying all of them and to distil and present a practical guide to awakening, also called enlightenment or self-realization.

Based on Enza's own experience, *Instant Presence* demystifies ancient spiritual teachings and practices from East and West and reveals that spiritual enlightenment is not a faraway dream, but the ever-present reality always available here and now.

"The truth I talk about is not limited to any tradition," says Enza Vita, "but is found in, and open to, all true traditions".

For more information, please visit: www.enzavita.com

WATKINS

Sharing Wisdom Since
1893

The story of Watkins dates back to 1893, when the scholar of esotericism John Watkins founded a bookshop, inspired by the lament of his friend and teacher Madame Blavatsky that there was nowhere in London to buy books on mysticism, occultism or metaphysics. That moment marked the birth of Watkins, soon to become the home of many of the leading lights of spiritual literature, including Carl Jung, Rudolf Steiner, Alice Bailey and Chögyam Trungpa.

Today our passion for vigorous questioning is still resolute. With over 350 titles on our list, Watkins Publishing reflects the development of spiritual thinking and new science over the past 120 years. We remain at the cutting edge, committed to publishing books that change lives.

DISCOVER MORE . . .

Read our blog

Watch and listen to
our authors in action

Sign up to
our mailing list

JOIN IN THE CONVERSATION

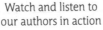 WatkinsPublishing    @watkinswisdom

 watkinsbooks    watkinswisdom   watkins-media

Our books celebrate conscious, passionate, wise and happy living.
Be part of the community by visiting

www.watkinspublishing.com